THE AUTOBIOGRAPHY OF DAVID WHITEHEAD OF RAWTENSTALL
(1790-1865)

David Whitehead.

THE AUTOBIOGRAPHY OF DAVID WHITEHEAD OF RAWTENSTALL (1790-1865)

Cotton Spinner and Merchant

Edited with an Introduction by
STANLEY CHAPMAN
University of Nottingham

HELMSHORE LOCAL HISTORY SOCIETY
2001

Text preparation by Hudson History,
Settle, North Yorkshire, BD25 9DZ

Designed, printed and bound by Smith Settle Ltd,
Ilkley Road,
Otley, West Yorkshire, LS21 3JP

ISBN 0 906881 10 2

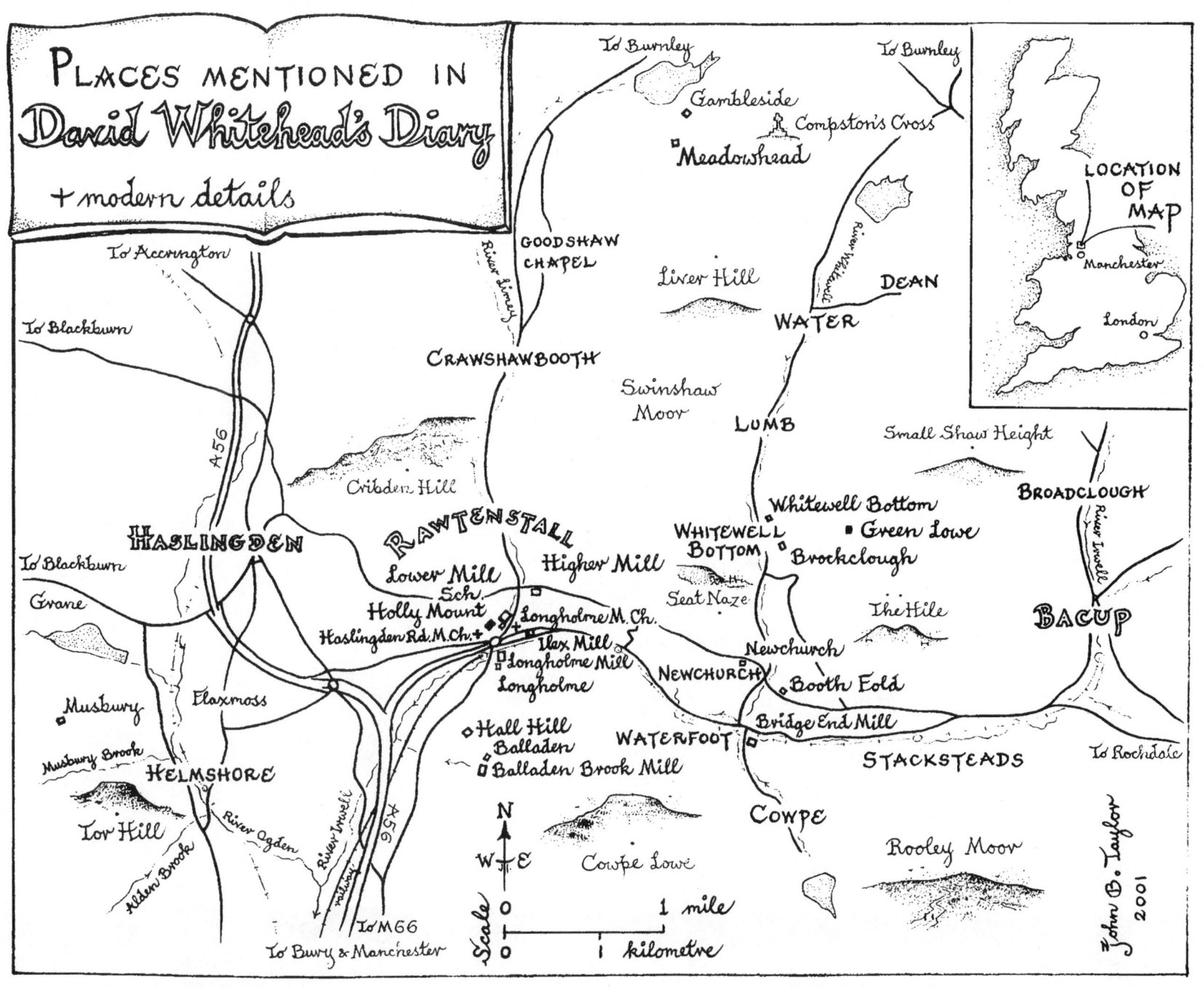

CONTENTS

Editor's Introduction	i
Preface to the Original Manuscript	1
The Autobiography	1
Early Years	3
Post Boy	16
Militia Man	19
To Chester	22
Back to weaving	25
Waiter in Wales	28
Wanderer's return	31
Inheritance	32
Joins Methodists	37
At Balladenbrook	40
Thomas Whitehead & Brothers	43
Betty Wood	48
Expansion of the Mill Enterprise	55
Methodist Class Leader	58
Rawtenstall Higher Mill, 1822-24	60
Longholme Chapel, 1826	61
The Hall Hill estate	65
Teetotal resolution	74
Cotton prices	77
Power loom riots	78
Methodist revival	87

Yorkshire Tour	90
Canadian Merchants	98
Parliamentary Elections	100
Holly Mount	106
Wesleyan Methodist dispute	108
Lower Mill 1833	110
Miser Holt	117
Lower Mill 1840	122
Free Trade	125
Higher Mill fire	126
Letters to Jonathan	127
The Plug Drawing Riots	136
Anti-Corn Law League	137
New Longholme Chapel	144
Anti-Corn Law League	148
Correspondence on Education	153
The 1848 crisis	165
The Peace Society	171
The Wesleyan 'fly sheets' controversy	172
Divisions in the Wesleyan Bacup circuit	179
Sixtieth Birthday, 11 Dec 1850	182
Justice of the Peace	184
Notes	184
Letters of David Whitehead and Betty Wood	186
Index	204

ACKNOWLEDGEMENTS

Helmshore Local History Society wish to thank:

Rawtenstall Library for permission to publish David Whitehead's diary and letters.

Professor Stanley Chapman for editing the manuscript and providing an introduction.

The Millennium Festival Awards for All programme for a generous grant towards the publication of the book.

Whitaker Park Museum, Rawtenstall for permission to reproduce the portrait of David Whitehead; and Mr. Edward Roberts for taking the photograph used on the cover.

Mr. John Taylor for preparing the map and a family tree.

Whitehead's spelling and punctuation have been amended slightly to make the diary more readable.

EDITOR'S INTRODUCTION

IT IS SURPRISING that David Whitehead's autobiography has never been published before. An abridged typescript prepared by H.I.Hunt in 1956 and retailed in Lancashire sold out very quickly. Clearly the work has much more than local interest for, apart from Robert Owen, it is the only autobiography of a major textile manufacturer written in the Industrial Revolution period. Moreover it is the work of a candid entrepreneur exploring and explaining his life and ideas on business, society, religion and politics without cant or pretence. While so many biographies and hagiographies pretend their subjects to have risen from the lowest ranks of society, scarcely mentioning the good fortune of education, connection or inheritance, Whitehead is evidently a genuine instance of a man who struggled to reach the top with few connections and minimal education. Crouzet's analysis of the careers of 97 successful textile manufacturers active in the century 1750-1850 shows that only four were originally workmen of any kind, while Howe's[1] study of *The Cotton Masters 1830-1860* stresses the hereditary nature of the industry's leadership. Research has produced some substantial works on the pioneers of the cotton industry (Peel, Arkwright, Oldknow, Greg, McConnel & Kennedy and others) but the struggles of the second generation, who missed the abnormal profits of the early years, have been largely neglected; we have only Sir Rhodes Boyson's *The Ashworth Cotton Enterprise 1818-1880*, which is a study of a farming and manufacturing family, as the author says, "in comfortable circumstances."[2]

While Whitehead records his ideas and aspirations in interesting detail, the facts given about the development and nature of his business are sometimes meagre, and he records little of his contemporaries. The main function of this short Introduction must therefore be to provide a few more details and sufficient context to explain the significance of various developments. There are very few other contemporary Whitehead records – only an account book of 1855-65 and an inventory of machinery made after Whitehead's death[3] – but a variety of other sources provide a little more substance and colour to the text.

David Whitehead spent a restless adolescence in the volatile trading conditions of the Napoleonic war. He was educated, as he explains, more by a variety of employment and company (from the beggar to the nobility) than by formal schooling. It was in this period that he embarked on a spiritual journey that took him from conversion to a position of prominence in the Wesleyan Church, and the absorption of his mind in religious issues occupies a substantial portion of the text. Consequently it was not until 1817, when he was already 26, that Whitehead and his brothers started their own little firm. They began with an old jenny worth about £3, spinning waste, surely the lowest rung of independence in the industry, and one from which few were able to maintain their independence for long. It was at this period that he walked the 20 miles to Manchester to buy raw cotton or to sell the brothers' yarns.

The real break came when Whitehead was able to negotiate a loan of £100 from Thomas Hoyle of Manchester, a Quaker and distant relative on his mother's side. In view of the crucial importance of this development, it is surprising that Whitehead does not say more about his patron's career. Hoyle had spent his early years working at Ardwick Bridge Iron Works (Manchester), where he presumably learned all about making equipment and machinery for the fast-growing cotton industry. In 1782 he started his own calico printing works at Hayfield, initially with only one machine to work, and with his son as partner. This experience must have given him the faith to invest in his young relative, who was struggling in similar circumstances. Thomas Hoyle & Co conducted their business "with good success" down to about 1828, when it was sold to new partners who went on to even greater achievements. It seems that the partners were already approaching the end of their business careers in 1817, another good reason for investment in a promising new enterprise.[4]

The Whitehead Brothers' first factory was Bridge End Mill (Waterfoot), which eventually had six throstles (288 spindles) and one weft engine (jenny). This was a small and relatively backward development for the period, for already in the 1780s Arkwright was licensing roller spinning mills of 1,000 spindles each, usually water powered and about 70 ft x 30 ft wide.[5] It is not surprising to learn that Bridge End was closed in 1824, when the economic boom allowed the brothers to build Higher Mill, Rawtenstall, with a steam engine, throstles, mules and power looms. The latter were quite a new development at the period, and still being stoutly resisted by some of the handloom weavers, as the riots of 1826 sharply reminded the brothers. We lack specific details of this particular concern, but it was probably much like that recommended by James Montgomery's well-known text for mill managers, with a 25 h.p. steam engine, 2160 throstle spindles, 2400 mule spindles and 28 power looms, costing some £12,000 in all.[6] Only eight power loom plants are mentioned in Whitehead's text, probably nearly the total in existence in north Lancashire at the period. Fielden Bros of Todmorden were lucky to escape attack and then built a much bigger loom shed in 1829.[7]

In this period Whiteheads became sufficiently prosperous for David to emerge as the "market man", the firm's specialist in buying raw cotton from their Liverpool broker and selling calicoes from their inn in Manchester. Liverpool cotton brokers formally stood as agents for the shippers, conducting all business with mill owners for them, but in reality were major figures in the port in their own right. On the three principal market days, but more especially on Tuesdays, great numbers of manufacturers from the neighbouring towns and 30 to 40 miles round Manchester flocked into town for the sale of cotton goods. To expose their goods for sale, the manufacturers hired rooms in inns and other buildings in the vicinity of the Market Place. In 1809 the first Cotton Exchange was completed and became the centre at which manufacturers and merchants could meet. Membership of the Exchange rose quickly from 1,543 in 1809 to 5,579 in the year of Whitehead's death (1865).[8]

From 1780 onwards a number of ambitious cotton manufacturers strove to become merchants, selling their goods directly to overseas branches or agents. At the peak of this activity, in the mid-1790s, some 60 Lancashire firms took this path, but few indeed were able to keep to it during the difficult trading conditions of the French Wars. The revival of trade after the post-war depression renewed interest, but even wealthy firms like Philips, Wood & Co. and Robert Gardner & Co. did not survive many years in the dual capacity. It is not surprising to learn that David Whitehead's firm failed with their Canadian export business. The only firm of spinners and weavers to make a substantial fortune as exporters was Fielden Bros., and they only did so by acquiring a finance house in Liverpool and New York that was able to keep a tight rein on the credit of their American customers.[9] Starting as merchants with only £3,000, Whiteheads lost a lot of money in Canada through bad debts. £30-40,000 capital proved insufficient to run this overseas trading operation, and the venture was finally wound up in 1841. David Whitehead's fixed capital at his death in 1865 was £59,000, and his total capital probably not more than £100,000, while that of Fieldens was already six times as much and rising steadily. The earliest surviving ledger, for 1855-65, shows David Whitehead following the established trade practice of selling goods for both the domestic and overseas markets through Manchester merchants, in his case largely through an old friend trading as John Munn & Co. Only a trickle of goods went direct to local calico printers.[10]

However, this is to move ahead of the chronology. In the upswing of the trade cycle in the early 1830s, the brothers turned to further expansion, and they bought an estate with a few cottages and an old mill at Rawtenstall. For the rest of the decade they employed 40 or 50 men in building the mill, three houses known as Holly Mount for the brothers to live in, 80 workers' houses, a handsome school (1839) and Methodist chapel, all close to Rawtenstall Lower Mill. There has been so much written on early factory colonies that it would be easy to suppose that they were typical of the period rather than ventures of exceptional entrepreneurs. A government inquiry of 1833 suggests that less than 10 per cent of cotton spinners had so much as a few cottages attached to their mill.[11] When W. Cooke Taylor visited the site in 1842 he was most impressed with the quality of all he saw:

> "The mill ... is one of the most extraordinary architectural works in Lancashire. A river flows beneath its arched floor, and has necessitated an expenditure of nearly as much building below as appears above the surface ... The machinery exhibited all the latest refinement of mechanical ingenuity ... The village of Holly Mount would elsewhere be called a thriving town. The residences of the operatives are not so much cottages as handsome houses consisting of from four to six rooms, provided with every convenience necessary for comfort and cleanliness. They are all well furnished – in many cases with mahogany: I saw none destitute of a clock and a small collection of books, generally on religious subjects ... The school attached to the factory was one of the most elegant and convenient buildings I have ever seen devoted to the purposes of education ... Messrs. Whitehead ... took me to see the chapel which had been erected in Holly mount, a building of the Ionic order, ... one of the prettiest specimens of the modern imitations of Grecian architecture I have ever seen."[12]

Though some allowance may need to be made for the fact that Cooke Taylor was sponsored by the Anti-Corn Law League, of which the Whitehead's were enthusiastic members, it remains true that their building achievement was quite extraordinary. The handsome Longholme Chapel, palatially built at a cost of £5,000 to seat up to 1,500 worshippers, still stands, its proportions offering a challenge to Rawtenstall parish church close by. The brothers' three fine Georgian houses (Holly Mount) have also survived, their proud position a reminder of the mill hierarchy. The standard dwelling of the Lancashire cotton mill worker at the middle of the nineteenth century had improved greatly within a couple of generations, but still consisted of no more than a parlour, kitchen, and two bedrooms, so Whiteheads' workers were particularly well housed.[13] The Holly Mount community was a show piece of the age in which the brothers invested their profits for several years.

Nevertheless, Whiteheads' wages were not particularly high. A government factory commissioner worked out in 1833 from the returns of 151 spinning mills in Lancashire and Cheshire that the average wage in the mill was 10s 5¼d, with significant variations across the region. Whiteheads' average was 9s. 6½d, higher than the Bolton average of 9s 3½d, but lower than those in the Manchester-Salford area. Average wages of a family living in Whiteheads' works cottages was 33s 0¼d, again lower than some other well-known firms.[14]

Cooke Taylor was accompanied on this visit by George Binns Ashworth, one of the cotton manufacturing family of Turton (Bolton) prominent in the Anti-Corn Law League. Ashworth made some private notes which add interesting details to the publicist's fulsome commentary. Lower Mill already had 500 power looms at work in 1842, with space for 800. They and the self-acting mules were activated by two steam engines of 60 h.p. each. The mill output was evidently popular rather than "up-market" as the mules were spinning coarse-gauge 22s, while (in Ashworth's words) the brothers' "weaving was not in any way remarkable, they were making domestics." The three Holly Mount houses were built on a high piece of ground, looking down on the mill and loom shed, with the chapel standing opposite their gates and the school adjoining the loom shed.[15]

The Whiteheads built a combined (or vertically integrated) mill enterprise, that is one with spinning and weaving on the same site. David Whitehead notes that his firm had a thousand looms by 1848, twice that in 1842, which made it a colossus of its day as the average weaving shed in 1850 had only 160 power looms and an economical type of combined mill recommended by Montgomery in 1840 had only 128 looms. At the top end of the scale, Fielden Bros. of Todmorden had 1,600 looms in 1856. Whitehead does not record the number of throstle and mule spindles his firm installed, but, pro rata, one would expect over 16,000 of the former and 18,000 of the latter.

Combined mills were widely built in the 1830s and 1840s for coarse spinning and plain weaving but became less characteristic of Lancashire's, the medium and fine branches of the cotton industry grew proportionately stronger. As the century advanced, economies of scale required bigger spinning mills but allowed small specialist weaving sheds to be viable.[16]

Possibly the most interesting feature of Whitehead's text is the exposure of the religious ideology which lay behind the commitment to business and to community building. Of the other major entrepreneurs featured in Cooke Taylor's book, the Gregs of Styal and the Ashtons of Hyde were Unitarians while the Ashworth Bros. were Quakers, and all three came of established wealth. Whitehead shows how first generation Wesleyanism could blend as easily with the new manufacturing system.

Wesley's famous sermon on the use of money enjoined his followers to gain all they could by honest means and then to save and give away all they could, and this finds an echo in some of Whitehead's letters to his son quoted at length in the autobiography.[17] While the son is enjoined to be diligent in his business to make himself fully master of it, he is reminded in the next letter of the practical and moral dangers of single-minded devotion to money making:

> A good tradesman should never desire to be rich – a wise one never will – but should do all he can honestly with his own capital to get all the money he can; a wise one certainly will. The next thing is to use the money when got in the best way, as he must give an account in the last day. A part must be devoted to religious purposes … the whole of the rest should be used for charitable and useful purposes.

The charitable work that Whitehead saw as his particular calling was "educating and enlightening the poor ignorant people, and to give labouring men employment." In a word, industrial enterprise and labour direction was an exercise in Christian charity. The greatest vice was betraying that Divine commitment by over-exposure of the business to commercial crises by taking too much credit.

Whitehead could easily take this simple view because he was so sure of his own Divine vocation. "Trade and commerce I still pursue with delight ... I am quite convinced I am in the way providence designed for me" he writes on one occasion, and on another "I believe I am in the business in which God intended I should be". This "blessed assurance" (the phrase is deliberately Wesleyan) gave the Whitehead brothers not only a simple direct faith but also, resting in the assurance of God's providence, a calm mind through the difficult trading conditions of the 1840s. Success of course brought more assurance that the brothers were in God's way and the Holly Mount community at Rawtenstall stood as a witness to the efficacy of the Wesleyan Christian virtues.

The pages of Whitehead's autobiography that focus particularly on his economic ideas (pp. 187-200 of the original text) cannot claim any great originality. They are set in the context of the commercial crisis of 1847-8 which he quite fairly blames on the railway mania and its effects, and on the Bank of England.[18] Whitehead's economic ideas were quite explicitly based on Adam Smith's *Wealth of Nations* and its liberal following, particularly Edward Baines of Leeds. Possibly the most interesting point that emerges here is that he discards Jabez Bunting and the Methodist luminaries of his age, preferring to be guided by his own business experience and Manchester School economic rationalism. Whitehead seems particularly heartless about the sweated labour of the East London tailoring workshops, striving to rationalise the behaviour of the notorious R. Moses & Sons, even though it is very doubtful that he knew anything about the firm or its industry.[19]

The most instructive part of the pages on economic issues is where Whitehead considers what may be called prudent business policy. He sets out to elucidate his ideas in abstract terms in the manner of the textbooks of political economy, but it quickly becomes clear that he is describing his own experience. So when he writes of 'A' who has a capital of £60,000 (£50,000 in a cotton mill and machinery, £10,000 floating capital) there is no question that he is rehearsing his own experience. The long-term success of Thomas Whitehead & Brothers is explained by the firm living entirely off its own resources, and more particularly, declining overtures from capitalists like 'B' whose speculations could bring several attendant firms to bankruptcy during the recurrent periods of financial crisis. The reports of the Manchester agent of the Bank of England confirm that there was much substance in Whitehead's remarks, except that taking the Lancashire cotton industry as a whole, the emphasis might be more on large firms becoming insolvent through overextending their credit in export markets (as Whiteheads nearly did in Canada) while small firms were particularly vulnerable to what became known as "slaughter houses" – capitalists who would offer to support struggling enterprises by taking their output at less than prime cost until their bankers became alarmed at a continually growing deficit and duly withdrew support.[20]

REFERENCES

1. F. Crouzet, *The First Industrialists. The Problems of Origins* (Cambridge, 1985); Anthony Howe, *The Cotton Masters 1830-60* (Oxford, 1984), chapter I.
2. Rhodes Boyson, *The Ashworth Cotton Enterprise 1818-80* (Oxford, 1970).
3. The surviving Whitehead business records are in Rossendale Museum.
4. John Graham, 'History of Printworks from 1768 to 1846', ms, Manchester Public Library.
5. S. D. Chapman, 'The Arkwright Mills', *Industrial Archaeology Review VI* (1981-82) 5-27.
6. J. Montgomery, *The Cotton Manufacture of the U. S. A.* (Glasgow 1840), pp. 114-7.

7. S. A. Weaver, *John Fielden and the Politics of Popular Radicalism 1832-1847* (Oxford 1987), p. 24.
8. Joseph Aston, *Picture of Manchester* (1816), pp. 206-8, 218; D. A. Farnie, 'An Index of Commercial Activity: the Membership of the Manchester Royal Exchange 1809-1948', *Business History XXI* (1979).
9. S. D. Chapman, *Merchant Enterprise in Britain* (Cambridge 1992), pp. 66-68. See also Brian R. Law, *Fieldens of Todmorden: A Nineteenth Century Business Dynasty* (Littleborough, 1995).
10. Rossendale Museum, Whitehead mss.
11. S. D. Chapman, 'Workers' Housing in the Cotton Factory Colonies 1770-1850', *Textile History VII* (1976) 130.
12. W. Cooke Taylor, *Notes of a Tour of the Manufacturing Districts of Lancashire* (1841), pp. 61-5.
13. A. B. Reach, *Manchester and the Textile Districts in 1849* (ed. C. Aspin, Helmshore, 1972), pp. 2-11, 65-7, 93, 100, 115.
14. R. Boyson, *op. cit.*, p. 104.
15. Rawtenstall Libraries and Museum, *Whitehead Mills Contemporary Description* (bound typescript, 1970).
16. D. A. Farnie. *The English Cotton Industry and the World Market 1815-96* (Oxford, 1979), pp. 284-6, 313-8; Manchester, John Rylands Library, Fielden mss; J. Montgomery, *op. cit.*, pp. 116-7.
17. John Wesley, *Forty-four Sermons* (1746-60), XLIV, 'The Use of money'.
18. D. Morier Evans, *The Commercial Crisis 1847-8* (1849), especially chapters I and II.
19. Moses & Son became notorious from Thomas Hood's poem 'Song of the Shirt', first published in *Punch,* Dec. 1843
20. S. D. Chapman, 'Financial Restraints on the Growth of Firms in the Cotton Industry', *Economic History Review*, XXXII (1979)

PREFACE TO THE ORIGINAL MANUSCRIPIT

I HAVE WRITTEN a rough sketch of a part of my life, though in a condensed form. Yet it is, I think myself, the most permanent part of my life, say, as far as I have written. It may be thought there are some things, little and simple; but let it be remembered that every river is so at its first start, some are much less than others when they empty themselves into the sea. But how large so ever they may become they were little at first, and I love to see the little beginnings of anything. I find in my life some things, which appeared most simple and little, have been of great importance in my after life a pearl besmeared with mud or covered with the shell showeth not its beauty. I am not a literary man, therefore nothing of that kind will appear. What I have written is like the rough granite stone, which I have neither time nor ability to polish.

David Whitehead
Holly Mount, Rawtenstall
[1850].

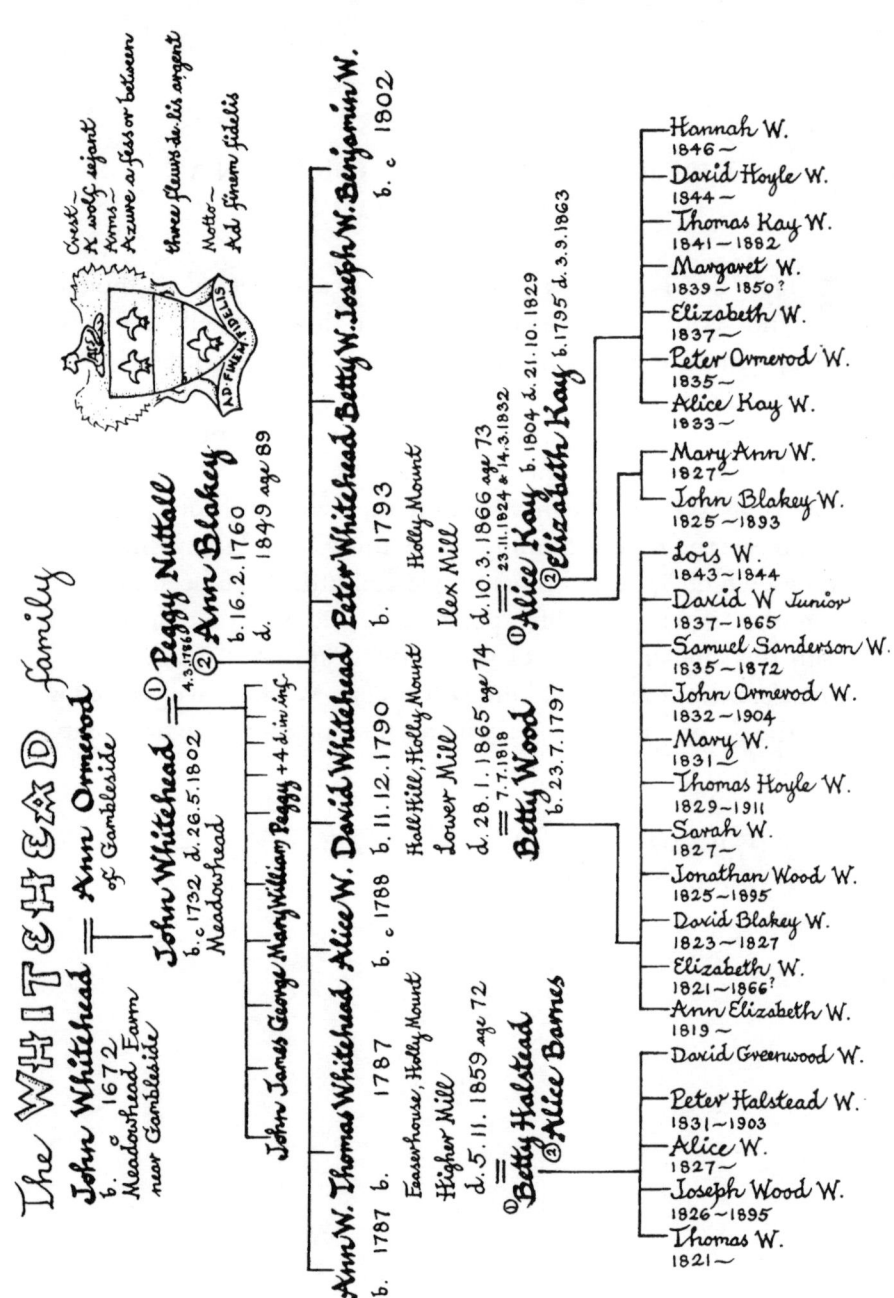

EARLY YEARS

I WAS BORN at Meadowhead, near Gambleside in the Forest of Rossendale, Lancaster, December 11th 1790. My father lived on his own estate which came to him by entail. He died May, 1802. He was about twenty-eight years older than my mother. He left her a widow with seven children, viz: Ann, Thomas, Alice, David, Peter, Betty and Benjamin, the youngest only one year and a half old. She was his second wife by whom he had eight children; and by his former wife, ten, of which at his death six of them were living, viz: John, James, George, Mary, William and Peggy. So he was father to eighteen children. He bequeathed his property to the thirteen surviving children and widow to be divided in the ratio of three pounds to males, to two pounds to females; and the widow to have fifteen pounds per annum to assist her to maintain herself and her seven children until the youngest child attained the age of twelve years; then his estate to be divided as above.

Soon after my mother was married to my father she began seriously to consider her responsibility both as regards domestic affairs and her soul's salvation; and those whom she had to watch over. Her soul was in deep distress for salvation. She heard of John Wesley and was determined to hear him preach, and soon had the opportunity. One time when she heard him preach at Burnley, some wicked people threw rotten eggs at him, at which she felt very much grieved, believing him to be a man of God. Afterwards she joined the Methodist Society. Some time after, my father also joined the Methodist Society.

After my mother was converted, she was rigidly strict with all her children; so much so that she would scarcely allow them to play with any other children except she was present. I can well recollect the time when I had never heard a profane oath sworn, and also the first time when I attempted to damn and curse. It was as follows.

One night I happened to be up later than usual when my father came home. In the course of his conversation with my mother he said he thought things or times were going to be worse, for James Ashworth (a woollen manufacturer) when taking in cloth, had been damning and cursing hard. Now I always thought, ever since I can recollect, that I would some time be a manufacturer. So the next morning I set my wits to work as to what was damning, which I thought I could manage. But I could not satisfy myself what was "cursing." However, there was a little running of water a little distance from the house. I got a quantity of sods and dammed up the water, and ordered my sister Alice to get some bits of cloth and bring them to me, to this water. I would be the Master and she should be the weaver; at the same time making up my mind that I would damn and curse over them. So when she brought them I said they were bad pieces, and that she must look at that water, for I was damning and cursing over them being so bad. Never having heard anyone damn and curse, I managed it as well as I could. My brother Peter and me were always planning some new thing or other in our play, making water wheels, setting them to work, and building little places for them to work in; sinking little places in imitation of coal pits; and sometimes we carried out our schemes a long way considering our age. Brother Thomas did not enter so much into our planning, but would often be watching us and sometimes helping a little. My mother has since told me that my father would sometimes take her to look what her two lads had been doing, and would have said, "I cannot tell what these two lads will be; or if anything should happen me, what you should do with them. I fear David will be like James – go to sea."

But my mind was never led that way. Brother James went to sea in a merchant vessel, and, after one or two voyages, when in Liverpool, in 1790, was pressed and taken into the naval army. He was with Lord Nelson in all his engagements at sea, and remained there after the death of Lord Nelson until the war was over – and never received a wound in any battle. When he had been twenty-four years at sea, he came home for a few months, and returned again; in a short time got his discharge, but died on his passage home.

At the death of my father, my mother left the farm and took her seven children to a cottage house at Brock Clough, a part of which she employed weaving; and had very hard to work herself, often all night. I have wakened in the night and heard her looms going "Tip-a-tap, tip-a-tap, tip-a-tap, tip-a-tap," and her praying, "Lord bless me, Lord bless me, Lord help me, Lord help me, Lord bless me..." etc.

Brother Peter and I went for a short time to a cotton factory. While working there, a strap caught me by my clothes; I seized hold of a machine and held fast, and cried out with all my might. The factory was stopped immediately. The overlooker came to me, and was so glad to see me alive, he dashed his hat upon the floor and said, "He is no more dead nor my hat!" and so made a joke of it, although I believe he was much alarmed. For if the mill had run a minute or two longer, I know not that I could have held on, and it might have been immediate death to me.

She [my mother] soon found we three brothers were fonder of scheming, planning and playing than weaving, so she thought she would get us to some trade or good place where we might have good training. Brother Peter she got to a farmhouse with John Holding in Musbury, brother Thomas with Mr. John Pickup, of Whitewell Bottom. I wanted to be a mechanic or a joiner, but as I was lightly built it was thought I had better be a tailor. So I was sent to Rochdale to learn to be a tailor, a trade which I thought I could never like. Through persuasion, I went a month on trial. At the expiration of the month, my mother and some friends came to Rochdale to bind me prentice. But all the duration of this month I thought I should not like to be a tailor, and as they were come, and just ready to knit me too fast, as I thought, and while they were in conversation with my master – I was in the room above, and heard my Master say he liked me very well but it was a custom with him to ask the boy if he liked the trade. Whereupon he called me down into the room, and asked me if I was willing to be his apprentice, and if I liked the trade. I said at once I did not like the trade, and should not like to be bound prentice. He said he would not take me as he had made up his mind he would never have an apprentice who did not like the trade. They were all amazed, and wondered what I meant. My master and family were very respectable, and Wesleyan Methodists, which made it so much greater disappointment to my mother. She took me out and advised with me, but could not prevail of me to alter my statement. First one and then another advised with me until I was completely weared out, so I plainly told them they might as well never talk, for I should not alter from what I had said. So there was an end to this business.

I came off home with my mother with a light heart, though I did not show it. But I believe my mother was the reverse, and when we got home she told me that I should not live at home, and looked very much displeased at me.

Soon after, she got me to a place to learn to weave fustian, and I lived there about eight or nine months, and was kept very well at my work, which was to milk morning and night, and weave fustian the rest of the day. This I liked better than being a tailor, though I was confined very close at my work. Most likely I should have lived there longer, but one night my Master told me I drank the new milk when I went to milk the cows, of which he said I made a common practice. At this I was astonished, and said I was certain that I never did such a thing in all my life. He told me he knew I had done it, and said if I denied it, he would knock me from the table. I was innocent, but durst not speak. This was at supper, and a supper it was for me! But I did not eat any more of it, but got up from the table and did not speak another word. Being near bedtime, I went to bed, but not to sleep, for sleep I could not. My head was full of thought and my heart of trouble; I could not imagine how he could think such a thing of me.

At length tears began to flow freely, which gave me much ease. Then I thought "As soon as they are all gone to sleep, I will get up and go home." Which I did, and got home very early in the morning, which rather alarmed my mother, who wanted to know what was the matter. I explained the whole; she said I had done quite right to come home, and that I might live at home if I would be good and mind my work as at other places. I said I would, and was glad she would let me. In a few days she went for my clothes and took me with her. She asked my master what reason he had for thinking that I drank the new milk. "Well", he said, "Suppose he might make a practice of drinking a pint or three gills every morning and night, I do not think it would be much loss for he would eat so much less."

This did not satisfy my mother; she wanted to know what reason he had for thinking I drank the new milk. He said he had told his son (about eight years old) to watch me; who told him he saw me drink the milk, and that he should believe his son. My mother said she did not believe me to be guilty of the charge. He said he did not mind if I did drink the milk, I might stop again if I had a mind. I told him I would not stop again upon any terms, and that I would have my clothes and go home with my mother.

When I had been at home a short time I began in my old way, planning some new thing or other, and neglecting my weaving. My mother began to think it would be better to get me to some other business. She met with a man who said he would take me and teach me to weave flannels, if it was agreeable to her. But he said he should like me to be bound two or three years, as he should have some trouble in teaching me. But he said I might go a few weeks first to see how I should like. My mother said, "David, will you go with this man?" As I was always fond of learning and seeing something fresh, I said, "Yes, I will go." "Very well," said my mother, "I have no objections, he may go with you."

So I went, and took a bed with me, and he was glad that I was so willing to go with him. When I first went to his house the Master and Mistress were very friendly with me, and I could do nothing wrong. But after a little time they began to be not quite so friendly, and I strove to please them as well as I could. But all that did not avail anything, for they seemed to me to be more disagreeable everyday. I could not tell what was the reason except I was so dull in learning my business, for I could do nothing right.

But shortly after, a circumstance happened which caused me to think I had some enemy at work. My master's brother had suffered some loss in his cattle, I think the death of a cow. He wanted my master to go a-begging for him that he might make up the loss. My master went and another man with him. On their return they counted the copper, which amounted to about thirteen or fourteen shilling worth of copper, which they put into a new tin kettle which my Master had brought back with him. And I saw him put the kettle with the copper in it into the cloth press, not giving any further thoughts about it. But the day following, my Master and Mistress went to her mother's and left me in the house. At night my Master came home sooner than I expected, and when he had sat a little by the fire, he said, "David, go and fetch the copper that is in the kettle." I got up and went right to the cloth press, and looked there but could not find it. He said very hastily, "Bring it here I say!" I replied, "I cannot find it." He said, "You know where it is, and I'll make you find it." I said, "The last time I saw it, I saw you put it in here, and now I cannot find it in." "You know where it is," said he, "At the back of yonder stone in the milk house."

I stood astonished in the house, thinking whatever he could be about. But however, I went into the milk house, knowing that there was a large stone rearing up to the wall. I looked at the back of this stone and found the tin kettle with the copper in it. I brought it to him, not saying anything. He counted it over and said no more about it. But I had many serious thoughts, and began to suspect that he thought I was not honest.

Afterwards I was informed that his mother-in-law had told him that she had been informed by some of the family where I had lived at last, that I was not honest, that I had taken two pence off the clock head and was guilty of drinking new milk when I went to milk the cows. This I thought would be taken for truth, she being the next door neighbour to where I had lived. The same boy who told his father that he saw me drink the new milk told me himself that he took the two pence off the clock head and hid it in a wall until such time as he could spend it for his own pleasure.

I have no doubt but these reports had made a very unfavourable impression on the mind of my Master and Mistress, for I was very badly used for a few weeks. One night I was playing with some other boys in the yard before the door, and about ten o'clock I went to the door and found it was bolted. I stepped a little back from the door, and stood a little while considering which way would be best for me to do. After which I went into a neighbour's house, and told them that I was made out and could not get into the house. The woman of the house said "That is a bad job."

All the family seemed to be sorry for me. They said I might sleep on the couch chair. I accepted the offer and was very much obliged to them. When the family were gone to bed, I took the couch chair intending to sleep upon it. But I soon found that to sleep was out of the question, there were so many of those little nimble blood suckers, fleas; I was constantly fidgeting and turning, and the old couch chair cracking. It being midsummer they were quite alive. But early in the morning I left the house, and found my Master's door was unbolted.

I went in; it being Sunday morning I washed and dressed myself in my better clothes. Breakfast time came but little was said, only Master said, "Why did you not come in last night when I got up and opened the door?" I said little, most likely it was after I had got into the other house.

I went over home that day and would have told my mother all about it, but she would hear little of what I had to say. She told me to go back and strive to be a good boy, and said I ought to be in the house sooner at night; and wished me to take care to do everything I could to please my Master and Mistress, and would not allow me to say anything about their behaviour to me.

After receiving this advice I went back again. On my return, very little was said to me. The following week they were very cross with me, particularly my Mistress. She used me badly. Sometimes I thought my Master was rather in favour of me. Soon after, my mother came over, thinking to make an agreement with my Master about me learning the business. When she came, my Master was not at home; she began to talk with my Mistress about me, and, making some inquiry, in a very short time my Mistress began to use bad language to my mother, saying, "You are a lying woman." This I heard, being in the room above, but the principal part of their discourse I did not hear. My mother said, "From what I have seen in you he shall not stop any longer," and inquired where she could find the Master. My Mistress told her. She went to him and told him I must live no longer with him, and gave him to understand how she had been treated by his wife. He said, "I am very sorry, but I hope we shall make it up again." So he came with my mother to his house, after which he said, "Now I hope you will let him stop again."

My mother said, "No, he shall not stop any longer!" and ordered me to find my hat. I knew then it was a settled thing, for I never knew her break her word. So I went up into the chamber for my hat. My Master followed me and spoke very kindly to me, and desired me to come again, and asked me if I would. He spoke so kindly and intreated me so hard that I almost promised him that I would. As I was going home with my mother, I told her what had passed betwixt my Master and me. But she gave me to understand very soon that I must live no longer there. She said, "You shall go and live with your brother John." We went to his house. He said he could do with me, and would teach me to weave woollen bed quilts. This suited me very well, for in the short time I had been learning to weave flannels, I got a fair insight into that business, and was glad to learn something else. My mother, brother and I went back for my clothes and the bed. When we got there they said very little to us, but gave us my clothes and the bed. We brought them to my brother's house. I lived with him near two years. After I had learned to weave that kind of cloth, I had very little liking to it, as I generally felt very little interest in any kind of work after I had learned it. (But I was very fond of learning to read and write).

While living with my brother I went to the Wesleyan Sunday School, but often broke the Sabbath in coming home on Sunday evenings. I got more into loose company than I had done before. I have often thought that religious people who send their children to Sunday School should go with them, and help to teach, and come back with them. If not, they may not expect their children to have a good religious training. They should also take them to divine worship whenever their place of worship is open.

But to return: I was intent of learning to read and write, and applied my time this way at nights and other times when I could, which I was more attentive to than my work. I have no doubt but my brother had some trouble to get me on with my work. He was a very pious man and so was his wife, both Wesleyan Methodists.

But she had her failings; she indulged one of her sons very much, one whom she loved more than any of the rest of her children, after which he was a great source of trouble to her. I have heard her tell him, when he has been doing something which ought not to be done, that she would acquaint his father of it. And have seen him shake his fist in her face and tell her, "Do, if you dare!" So religious parents, if they allow their judgement to be governed by their passion, do not train up their children in the way they should go. The fruits of this neglect are sorrow and trouble in old age.

One day my brother and his wife both went from home and left the children and me in the house. Miss Ormerod had a servant girl who often came with her sewing, and who was very friendly with my brother's wife. She brought her sewing and was a good while in the house that day in their absence. It was found afterwards that a guinea had been taken out of the drawer. My brother's wife came up into the chamber where I was weaving, and said that I had stolen the guinea. I was quite innocent and in great distress in my mind on account of the charge. I said, with tears in my eyes, "No, I have not taken it. I never have seen it."

She was quite in a fury and said, "Come John, and beat him until he tells what he has done with it." My brother said very little, only if I had taken it he wished me to tell him. I told him I had not taken it. He saw that I was in very great trouble and said no more to me at that time. I went home to my mother and told her. She said, "David, you have not taken it have you?" I said, "No! No!, mother, I have not!" My mother was very much troubled, and went back with me and told them she believed I had not taken the guinea. My brother's wife said, "Oh!, but he has," and said I would not tell the truth about it. My brother asked them to say no more about it at present, and said, "Perhaps it may be found again." My mother said, "I hope you will find it, for I believe he has not taken it."

I went to my work again. In a few days after, my brother said in very kind way, "Come, David, tell me where the guinea is and I will give you something." I said, "John, how can I tell you where it is when I never knew where it was?" I was in great distress to think that my brother should doubt my word. He saw that I was in great trouble over it. He said no more. I was given to understand afterwards that he believed I had not taken it. I received many hints of it from his wife, which made it very unpleasant living.

One day, when my brother was from home, Miss Ormerod's servant girl came and brought her sewing with her as she often did, and after she had been talking some time with my brother's wife in the house, she called to me in the chamber above, saying, "Oh David! If I was them I would make you find the guinea!" I made no reply, but a thought struck my mind at the time, thus, "I should not be surprised if someone should tell me that you have taken it yourself," recollecting that she had often been left in the house by herself.

I lived with my brother about a year after this, but his wife firmly believed that I had taken the guinea, in consequence of which she could not think well of me, and I was not very favourable towards her. Altogether, it was very disagreeable, and I thought it would be better for me to remove and get some other place. I went and acquainted my mother of my intentions. She said she could not do with me at home, for she had not the conveniences. (My mother has since told me that my brother John's wife, a considerable time after this, told her that they had found out that David had not taken the guinea, but that Miss Ormerod's servant girl had taken it and had bought a new gown with it. While telling my mother, she wept very much, and was very sorry that she had for ever charged me with it).

I immediately went in search of a place for myself and got one that night with John Tattersall of Greenlaw. I was to weave Bockings, a kind of woollen base [baize], and help him in the farm. I got so well up to weaving these backings that one day I told my Master I thought I could weave faster than he could. He thought not. I told him I would try him against time, which could weave a yard soonest. He agreed, and he would weave the first yard, which he did in twenty minutes. Then I wove a yard in one minute less.

I did not live long at this place. They were very kind to me and I liked the place very well, but it happened one day that I had damaged my piece in some part of my weaving. My Master was very angry over that (or something else). I thought the damage was only a little one, but he was a passionate man, and in his haste said I must weave no more. I did not say anything, but in a little time began to try to weave, but he stopped my looms and said I should not weave anymore there. I sat a while in the looms, considering what to do. In the meantime my Master left me. But I began to think that as he had said so much I would not stop any longer. So I went and washed myself, and went home and told my mother. She had then removed from Brockclough to Boothfold. She seemed rather inclined for me to live at home. I was glad of that and went immediately back for my clothes. My Master told me that he did not think of me leaving. He had been angry and spoke rash, and hoped that I would stop again. (But there is no place like home). I told him I could not stop again for I was going to live at home, so he paid me my wages, I got my clothes, and returned home.

On the road I thought I would be a better boy than when I was at home before. But I had not been at home long before I began to trifle, and neglect weaving, say cotton weaving. It seemed to me to be such a hard job because it was always the same over again, every day. I would like to be tackling or making something, reading or writing, say anything but weaving. My mother could not afford to keep me in that way, and she told me she would have me bound prentice to some trade. One day she got herself dressed up and told me she would go to Burnley, and try if she could not get me to some trade, and would have me bound prentice. I thought, "I am a great deal of trouble to my mother. I can do for myself, I will not be bound prentice."

After my mother was gone off, I washed and dressed myself in my better clothes. I was then between fourteen and fifteen years old. I thought would go and get a place in some town. I fixed upon Blackburn if I could not get a place on the road. I made up my mind that I would do something different than weaving. I thought I would try if I could get a job in some public house. I tried one as I went through Rawtenstall, but without success. I tried three in Haslingden, but could not succeed. In the last of these, as I was returning out of the house, three men who were drinking in a room, and who had heard me inquire for a place, called me into the room. They inquired where I came from. I told them Boothfold. They asked me where I thought of going to; I said, Blackburn. They said, "Let us give him each a penny." I thanked them and was glad, for I had no money with me. This raised my spirits a little. Although it was about four o'clock in the afternoon, I went on to Blackburn. When I got there the sun was just about setting. After entering the town as far as the bridge, I stepped up to a gentleman and asked him if he knew any place where they could do with a boy like me. He said he could not tell but, "They do employ such boys at the New Inn." I said, "Where is that?" He pointed with his finger and said, "That is the place, right before your face."

I went in at the front door straight forward into the bar where I found the Master of the house, along with another three or four gentlemen. I asked him if he had anything to do for a boy like me. He said, "What can you do?" I said, "Anything." He and the other gentlemen laughed most heartily. He said, "Whose son are you?" I said, "Widow Whitehead of Boothfold near Newchurch is my mother." He said, "Well, you are a fine looking boy of somebody's. Go down into the kitchen and I will see in the morning."

I was very glad to hear that, for had I not stopped here all night I could not tell where I might lodge. I thought, "Now as I have got lodgings, if he will not have me I will get a place somewhere tomorrow." But in the morning nothing was said to me, but they set me to work cleaning knives and forks, shoes and boots and other things. My mother says that John Hall, who kept the inn, was a very nice gentleman, and had a great deal more thought for her than I had at that time.

I had not acquainted any of our family where I was going nor what about. I had just this idea, that I had been a great deal of trouble to my mother, and that if I could do for myself it would be a great relief to her. But he (John Hall) thought that very likely I was an apprentice that had run away, and that it would be a deed of charity to keep me and write to my mother. Which he did, not saying anything to me. My mother was in great distress about me until she got his letter. She came over in about a week or two. My Master called me and took me into the room where she was, and said, "Do you know this woman?" I was surprised but very glad to see her. She asked me if I should like to stop. I said, yes I should, if it was agreeable to her and Mr. Hall. She wished Mr. Hall to take good care of me and agreed to leave me with him.

POST BOY

He had engaged to post the letter bags from Blackburn to Clithero, so I rode the post between these two towns about half a year. I sometimes got as much as fifteen shillings per week for myself with this and cleaning boots and shoes at night. So I was post boy and the "boots." I was desirous of making as much money of my place as I could. Different persons gave me parcels on the road, and from one town to another. I had no wages but what I got in this way, and cleaning boots and shoes, except meat and lodging. So I always took care to deliver my parcels well, and looked as pleasant as I could to all. When anyone asked me what was the carriage, I said, "What you please," and often they would give me more than I would have charged. I always took care to look pleasant and thank a person kindly for a little. I have sometimes thought, when I gave them such warm and pleasant thanks, that they looked as if they thought themselves that they had not given me enough. In this way I got a good many parcels, sometimes money parcels. [The people who were sending] these would often pay me something when they gave me the parcel, and would tell me not to charge anything to the receiver but to let them please themselves. This was my custom in all cases, so it was "What you please!" in these cases also. For such parcels I often got something at both ends, and therefore as I said before, I made some weeks as much as fifteen shillings. After my Master gave up the post which he did in about a half year after I went there, I could not make so much money.

We had a cook who was rather funny, and would often have a little sport with me. One night I thought I would have some fun with the cook, and knowing she was coming up into a chamber which I was in, I took a candle and placed it near the roof upon the wall. But when she came up she said nothing but went back and told the Master. He came and thought most likely that I was going to set the house on fire, for he took me and shook me and said, "What! Are you going to set the house on fire?" I thought the cook had done an injustice after being so playful with me. I felt as if my Master had lost his confidence in me, and did not stop long after this. I thought perhaps it would be better for me to have a trade and to be bound prentice. I knew a gentleman in Preston, one Mr. Liddle; he was well acquainted with my mother. I went to him and told him I wished to learn some trade. He knew a painter who wanted an apprentice and asked would I learn that trade. I had no objections. He went and agreed with the painter who also lived in Preston, for me to go on trial for a month or two. In the meantime he corresponded with my mother. This short time I was engaged in mixing paints, and painting, and though the time was short, I learned to letter so that I could letter a common sign board. The painter had a journeyman painter who taught drawing at nights. He gave lessons to his Master's apprentices without charge. So I went to drawing school at nights, and got some outline of the method of drawing, which altogether I liked very well. But whether my mother could not afford to give the fee or money the painter required, or she did not come over as soon as he expected, I cannot tell. But he told me to go to Mr. Liddle. I could not tell what was the matter, but I told Mr. Liddle if the painter did not want me, I knew a man who would have me (he was a cooper by trade).

Mr. Liddle said I might go and try him. I went and engaged myself with him until my mother came to Preston, which I thought would not be long. If he and my mother could agree, I had no objections to be his apprentice and learn the trade. So he set me to work and I thought I should like the trade, for I had a particular pleasure in making something new. In the course of a few weeks I could make a bucket very well. My mother came over to Preston with an intention to bind me prentice. My Master said I should do very well for him and was willing to take me as an apprentice; I was willing to serve him. But he said if he took me, he must have twenty pounds, say £20, with me. My mother said she was not able to give the money, so the business ended.

After visiting Mr. Liddle, my mother and I set out for home. On our way we called upon Mr. Hall of Blackburn, my former place. They were very friendly and kind to us and wanted me to stop with them again. To which I agreed, but didn't stay for more than a few months, after which I went home. My mother had then removed from Boothfold to Whitewell Bottom. She received me very gladly, and said she could do with me at home very well if I would be a good boy.

I shortly left home again, and went to live with George Ingham, near Rawtenstall. He was a good scholar in arithmetic. I got what lessons I could at nights. I was very anxious then to learn arithmetic. I lived with him about half a year. It happened that the family became most seriously affected with the itch. They could not tell how they had got it. I was so afflicted with it that I could scarcely do anything. My mother came and advised me to go home. I had given my mother a great deal of trouble, but she took good care of me and soon got me well again.

One day my mother said, "David, the clock goes very badly, get a feather and brush the dust out and oil it." I said, "I can manage that very well," for anything of that kind just suited me. My mother went to her weaving and I to the clock. When I began to brush the clock, I saw that I was brushing the dust into the pivots of the wheels, and was thereby doing more hurt than good. I thought, "I will take the clock down and take the wheels out, and give them a good cleaning," which I did, taking good notice how the wheels were connected. When I had got all the wheels out and was brushing and cleaning them, Mrs. Ashworth came in and called out to my mother, "What, Mrs. Whitehead, you have got the clock dresser!" My mother came into the room, said, "Whatever are you doing! My clock will be ruined." Mrs. Ashworth said, "Don't be alarmed, Mrs. Whitehead, he will not break anything. If he cannot manage it, you will only have to send for the clock dresser after all." So my mother let me go on. I put the clock together again. All was right. It went remarkably well, after which my mother would have me to be her clock dresser rather than anyone else.

I began then to be very diligent in learning to write and read and do arithmetic, but not so diligent at my work. I never did like to weave so if possible I thought I would make myself fit for something else. One day when writing instead of being at my weaving, my mother began to complain over me taking up so much time in writing. I held up my pen to my mother and said, "I mean to be able through my pen to keep you." She said, "You little good-for-nought! You keep me!" and at the same time could scarcely hold for smiling. She has often mentioned this to me since then.

I gave attention to my learning very diligently for about a year and a half. One day I entreated my mother very hard to let me go to school one quarter of a year. At last she consented for me to go, and she would see whether she could or not. But when I had gone for two weeks, she said she could not afford to let me go any longer. So I got on as well as I could myself, and when I was fast with a problem, I went to someone in the neighbourhood to set me right.

MILITIA MAN

About this time there was great talk about the French invading England and the inhabitants were either to volunteer or be lotted for the Local Militia. I had always had an objection to be a soldier and for fear of being lotted [allotted, i.e. conscripted] for the old Militia, I volunteered for the Local Militia, as the old Militia were in constant service, but the Local Militia were only to serve a month in the year. I was fond of music and wished either to play the fife or drum. So they made me into a drummer. Times were very hard for my mother, but I got two guineas for volunteering and when we were called out we had marching allowance to Blackburn and also back, which I saved, something out of my pay. I saved about a guinea in the month, which I brought home. But the company of fifers and drummers which I was billeted with were the wildest and most wicked set I ever joined in my life. They drank their money till they had to starve for food; they wrote to their parents for money and got money from them. I knew that my mother could not spare any money for me. We had what was called the "tommy" day (i.e. we had dealt out to us every few days, bread and beef and a little money). A great number of the party whom I was billeted with, as soon as they got to the inn, would roast their beef upon the fire and eat it, and most of their bread, and drink their money the same night.

But I took another plan. There lived a woman across the street who sold flour, potatoes, etc., and baked bread, pies, etc., for people. I went to this woman and said, "I want you to take this beef and let me have some flour and potatoes, as much as the beef will require, and make me a good size pie of it. And I want you to let it remain here, and I will come and eat it here as I need it." So I went everyday to get a little pie with the old woman, and if she wanted any little thing doing I did it for her, shifting her flour or potatoes, which pleased her very much. She seemed very glad to see me come in, and it was a very comfortable shop for me, and assisted me to save a little of my pay. But those of my party who had eat their beef and bread, and drunk all their money, came to me and wanted me to give them meat, or let them have money. I said, no, I would do-nothing of the kind. They cursed and swore at me, calling me a stingy devil, because I would not give them my money when they had drunk their own. I knew my mother would want all I could take her.

Trade continued very bad, and I did not like weaving, and I thought would if possible get something else to do. One day I said to my mother, "If you will give me five shillings, I will go to Manchester and try if I cannot get into some warehouse, or some other job than weaving." I thought I would call upon Mr. Thomas Hoyle, Calico Printer, who was a distant relation of my mother, and try if he could find me a place. He told me nearly all the mills in Manchester were shut up, and he saw no chance for me at present. I also called upon Mr. Jno. Munn, a commission agent, an old acquaintance of my father. He took me home with him, and I stopped with him a few days, but he could not find me any place. I tried every place I could think of, but could not get a situation. In about a week I returned home again and gave my mother the five shillings back, as I managed to get on without spending it. She was pleased and received me kindly.

I continued attentive to my writing and arithmetic, but not so in my weaving. My mother said she could not do with me doing so little work. I said "Well, will you give me the five shillings again, and I will try to get something else to do, for I do not like to weave." I thought I would go to Wales upon some of the main post roads and try to get to be a post boy, to drive a post chaise or ride postillion, but did not say to my mother what I intended to do. She gave me the five shillings; I set off about three o'clock in the afternoon and thought I would go to Manchester that night. When I got to Newhallhey Bridge, Rawtenstall, the coach was just before me. I called out, the coach stopped and I got on. When I was at Blackburn amongst the post boys and coach drivers I could often get on with them by giving sixpence or a shilling, and thought I could do so with this coach driver. But I could not make him understand me. He said the coach fare was 4s. 6d. and, if I would not pay him that, I must see them at the office. He left me in the street. I might have gone away, but this I could not do without settling with him or in the office. I went in and told them, as I had told him before, that I was going to Wales and had but five shillings. They said if I was going to Wales I had more than that, and I must pay four shillings. Which I did pay. I found I had missed my way, but I recollected I knew a coachman who was at the Star Inn in Manchester. I went to him and told him. He said, "Well,

David, thou hast missed it this time, but come, lad, I will find thee a bed." So he took me to Castle Inn and paid for my bed.

TO CHESTER

I got up early in the morning and started for Chester, having then only one shilling. I walked on a long way then I called at a farmhouse, and asked them if they would sell me a pennyworth of bread and milk. The good woman of the house brought me some. After eating the bread and drinking the milk, I gave her the penny and went on my way. I could not think of begging, so I adopted this plan, telling those who sold me food how much money's worth I wanted, leaving them to give me as much as they would; and I thought I got a good deal for the money.

When I got within about five miles of Chester there came on the road a returned chaise. I asked the driver if he would let me ride to Chester for four pence, to which he agreed. I told him I had little money and asked him if he could tell me where I could stop all night for a little. He said if I went through Chester there were some lodging houses over the bridge, where I might get to lodge for a little. He showed me the way.

It was now dark, and a very dark night. It had been a thorough wet day; my clothes were wet through. When I got to the other side of the bridge, as he had informed me, I called at a house and inquired for lodgings. There was a poor old woman sat at tea; she asked me where I came from. I told her and said I was going to Wales to try to get a situation, but had little money to support me on my way. She began to pray for Christ Jesus to bless me, and used her words so strangely I could not tell what to make of her. She asked me to have some tea which I accepted, and thanked her. She said she could not give me lodgings, but sent a little boy to show me where she thought could get lodgings.

They took me in, but it was a very strange house, and their ways seemed to me to be as strange. My clothes being so very wet I stripped a part of them off to be dried by the fire. The woman whom I took to be the mistress of the house thought that her two pigs were lost or drowned in the river, and appeared to be in great distress. There was another dirty woman seated at the other side of the fire, seemed as if she was laughing at everyone in the house. Shortly I heard an old woman with a very gross voice coming from some other part of the house D........ and swearing that the divel was in the chips for she could not light her fire. The dirty woman said, "Mrs. Green, what is the matter?" she coming slowly on and saying, "The divel is in the chips!"

I was almost frightened to hear the wicked old woman before I saw her. She came up to the fire and brought with her a tea cup and saucer. She was very dirty and her pots no better. She drank her tea out of those dirty pots. She wanted to borrow some salt. The other dirty woman alluded to before who sat at the other side of the fire had a little child on her lap. She said, "I will lend you a little salt, Mrs. Green." Pulling a little bag out of her pocket she took a little salt out betwixt her fingers and gave it to her.

Then there came two men into the house to apprehend two soldiers lodging there who they said had been stealing coals. I began to wonder what kind of a house I had got to. It was a large house, and I thought most likely they lodged soldiers, thieves, beggars and I know not what. They found me a bed; it was a coarse one which appeared to be clean. They charged me three pence for my lodgings which I paid. I went to an eating house and got a little breakfast. I think my money was near all spent.

There was one Mrs. Bury, who had formerly lived in Rossendale, then living at Ruthin in Wales, to which place I reached about teatime. I soon found Mrs. Bury, who entertained me very kindly and was very glad to hear of her old country. Her daughter was also with her. They inquired about everyone they could think of in Rossendale, and I told them all I could. They were highly pleased, and we passed a very pleasant evening.

My lodgings were splendid this night. What a difference betwixt this and last night! But she could not imploy me in any way. She asked me my reasons for leaving home. I said weaving was bad, and I wished to have some other employment. After breakfast she gave me six pence and directions to Mr. Weaver at Kernioge Moor Inn who kept a large inn on the great road from London to Dublin. He employed a great quantity of servants. I went direct to that place, but Mr. Weaver could not imploy me. But I had very great kindness shown to me there. I found his wife was a native of Rossendale and her father lived near to where I came from. I remained there two nights.

I got introduced to the post boys who allowed me to ride from one place to another in returned chaises. Mr. Weaver gave me a letter of introduction to Mr. Griphy [Griffiths?], who kept a large inn on the same road called Capel Curig. I went to Capel Curig and delivered my letter. I was handed into a room where there were two other gentleman's servants. The waiter shortly brought me supper. I asked him if he thought there was a vacant place for me. He said he thought not. In the morning I asked Mr. Griphy if he could give me any employment. He told me he could not. My hopes of getting a situation then was all over.

When I left home I believed I thought I would not return back again, but this had been such a tour as I had not had before, and every attempt to get a place seemed to be thwarted. I was so full of grief that I was very glad to get out of the presence of Mr. Griphy, that I could give vent to my feelings. I was handed down into the kitchen to take breakfast but could eat little for weeping. My mind was eased at once by coming to the conclusion that I would return home again.

I saw then how vain it was in me to think that I would not return home again. I was then a long way from home, and had very little money to carry me home, and not eighteen years old. But I made up my mind that I would get home as soon as I could, and would not try any more to get a situation. So I came back to Kernioge Moor in a returned chaise and stopped there all night. The next, morning I walked to Ruthin and remained there all night at the house of Mrs. Bury. In the morning she gave me a shilling and as much meat as I could put into my pocket. The next day I walked to Northwich, about forty miles. I slept at a public house. The day following I walked about forty miles and took up my abode for the night with an old acquaintance of my mother, about seven miles from home. The next day I arrived at home; my mother was very glad to see me back again, and I think I was very glad to see her; and I think I saw more of the value of a mother then than I had ever done before.

BACK TO WEAVING

I began then to be more diligent at my weaving, and when not at my work, improving myself in my books. Mr. Southerst of Haslingden was (what is generally called) a putter-out for Peels,[1] that is one who puts out warp and weft to hand loom weavers, and it is brought back in cloth; sometimes they are called takers-in. Mr. Southerst came to Whitewell Bottom to put out for Peels. He did not remain there long as it did not answer their purpose. But while he continued I assisted him in livering out and taking in for which I was very glad, as I always thought that I would be a cotton manufacturer.

After he left I took a little house and got my mother to let me have my looms. I began to sell a little of grocery and weave a little beside. Then I thought I would try hawken [hawking]. George Ingham with whom I lived sometime ago for half a year, now kept a drapery shop in Haslingden. He agreed to furnish me with goods if I would go a-hawken them.

While following this business I saw into many things which I did not know before. I found a many of weavers in country places, particularly in Pendle Forest, and Pickey [Pickup] Bank near Bellthorne who would often ask me if I took any white iron. By this they meant would I exchange my goods with them for weft which they had pilfered from their Masters.

I found one shopkeeper, a grocer, who wished to exchange with me some of this kind of weft for some of my goods. He had exchanged his groceries with the weavers for this kind of weft. This gave me to see how difficult it was for Masters to get their weft wrought up honestly, and brought back again. I found it very difficult to sell for ready money. People wanted to take goods and pay so much per month. If I took this plan I saw I should soon get a deal of money out in the country, and thereby be fast to this business, a business which I did [not?] much like. So I gave it up after a few months trial.

Then I thought I would begin to make a few pieces of calico myself. Mr. Ashworth, a neighbour, found what I was doing, said he would join me but he would be a sleeping partner, so I must not mention it to anybody. I agreed. When I went to buy weft and warp he would write a note with me to say I would pay for what I bought, or he would see that it was paid. Just after we had got to work, and before we had sold any goods Mr. Southerst came over to Mr. Ashworth and wanted him to go partner in the cotton trade, as he had left Peel's and was beginning for himself. Mr. Ashworth agreed and went partner with Mr. Southerst. Then Mr. Ashworth said, as he was going partner with Mr. Southerst, he would decline being partner with me, and would give me all the profit there might be since we began. Which I agreed to. After this, Mr. Southerst told me if I would come and assist him he would buy my pieces and he thought he could make me into a gentleman. So I sold him my stock and went to him. He had always given me on former occasions more than I could think of asking; so I left all this to his honour. After he had been manufacturing a few months, Peel's had been looking up his account of weft and warp delivered and received, and as there is generally a waste in livering out [delivering] weft, most likely he would be short on that item, but how it was I cannot tell. But I understood they brought an account against him, more than he could pay, so that he was sold up. And I think Mr. Ashworth lost something like three hundred pounds by him. I was very sorry for Mr. Ashworth, and Mr. Southerst too, whom I had every reason to believe to be honest. As I had made no arrangement for any wage, I could get nothing but what he had given me, which was very little. And as I had agreed to pay my mother a certain sum per week for meat and lodgings, my money was nearly all gone.

My brother Peter left Musbury and came home. We wove cotton and were both very diligent in self-education, but did not make very much progress, but what we did make proved very useful. One day, while in conversation with a young man in the neighbourhood about music, before we concluded, we agreed to try if we could establish a club in order to raise a band of music. We accomplished the object, and more than twenty members entered. But I think only about fifteen continued. We agreed to pay one shilling per week until we could raise as much money as would purchase such instruments as would be required for the band. And while we were raising the money, to imploy one of the Dean singers[2] to teach us to sing by notes in order to be able to read music when we got our instruments. My brothers Thomas and Peter were also members of the band.

I then threw my whole soul into the music line for I was very fond of music. We met once a week for singing and paying our subscription. After I had been learning a short time, I made a tune and harmonised it in four parts and took it to our teacher. He was well pleased with it but pointed out some errors. After that he gave me some rules how to harmonise music. The Dean singers were noted for making tunes. They attended the Baptist Chapel at Goodshaw, and mostly sung the tunes which they had made themselves. They were held in high repute as choral singers.

My brother Peter and I worked together and were very attentive both at work and studying music. We were not long before we got a part of the musical instruments. I was the leader of the band and played the first clarinet. We three brothers, Thomas, Peter and I were very true to each other, and had for some time the pleasure of enjoying each others company. But this was now broken off for about six months. (We had not then got all our musical instruments). Our separation was as follows.

WAITER IN WALES

I was informed that Mr. Weaver of Ceiriog Moor Inn in Wales wanted a servant man as waiter. His wife's father lived in the neighbourhood. I went to inquire of him if it was true. He said it was true. They wanted him to get them a man to be waiter at the Inn, and if I would go he would pay my fare to his daughter's house. My mother was then at Blackpool. I sent to her to know if I might go. She sent me a letter and consented for me to go. I immediately packed up my clothes; took the coach from Rawtenstall to Manchester, next morning from Manchester to Chester, from thence to Wrexham and then walked to Chirk, and from Chirk by the mail to Ceiriog Moor Inn in Denbighshire in Wales, where I arrived by four o'clock the next morning. A female servant got up and found me a bed. About ten o'clock the same morning I made my appearance to Mr. and Mrs. Weaver. I asked them if they remembered me being there about three years ago. They said they could recollect something about it. This inn was on the main road betwixt London and Dublin; the principal part of their company were the nobility and members of Parliament who often breakfasted or would stay for one night at this inn on their way to and from London and Dublin.

Mr. Weaver offered me the waiter's place if I would give him eighty guineas per year for the vails [gratuities], or if I would give up the vails to him he would give me after the rate of thirty guineas per year. As I had no knowledge what the place would make, I agreed take the thirty guineas; beside I had meat and lodgings.

We had no chance here of going either to church or chapel, but Mr. Weaver called all his servants together every Sunday and read the church prayers. While living here I had an opportunity of seeing some of the ways and doings of the higher class. This place was situated on a moor and appeared sometimes as if nobody would ever come near us; and perhaps in a quarter of an hour after, there would a great number of carriages and horses, and the house full of company.

One day Lord Auxbridge came. Before he arrived one of his servants came to announce that his lordship was on his way. We made preparations agreeable to his desire. His lordship came up with four servant men attending him. He was a plain old man, about eighty years old, very farmerly looking, but very polite. He was very well pleased with the house and would stay the night with us. He was well pleased with everything we brought him, and often said while I was waiting on him, "How nice everything is." When he left he gave me seven shillings for waiting. His steward brought me his shoes and wished me to get them cleaned, and said they must be blacked and glossed both tops and bottoms. I thought "I will clean these myself," so that I could say I had blacked his lordship's shoes, both tops and bottoms. He wore golloshes. His steward gave me two shillings and six pence for the boy who had cleaned his shoes. Everything I did pleased his lordship. And some family, whatever I did I could not please them at all, but we always set this sort down to be of a low kind. His lordship's servants came up in a few days after, about twelve in number, and three or four carriages. They took breakfast and went on, but they were a most jovial set. While at breakfast they would have the harp played, and while eating they were beating with their hands on the table to the tune, and with their feet upon the floor. As they say in Lancashire they were "over kept and under wrought," and appeared not to know on whose legs they walked.

We sometimes had as many as twenty families sleeping in the house in one night. A Welsh harper was kept in the house, and I have seen him play the harp on these occasions while the blood has trickled out of his finger ends. I had my clarinet with me but had little time to play upon it.

After a gentleman had gone to bed, when tidying up the room in which he had been sitting, I found a one pound Bank of England note. I told my Master that I believed it belonged to the gentleman who had been in the room that night. He told me to ask him in the morning which I did. The gentleman said it was his note, who gave me a shilling.

Another night, after I had taken a gentleman's boots off, I found a shilling in them. I acquainted my Master; he told me to go and give the shilling to the gentleman, which I did after acquainting the gentleman where I had found it, and left the room. Presently he rang the bell, to which I attended, and he gave me the shilling. I afterwards thought it was providential that I had acquainted my Master with the circumstances, for soon after there happened to be one night a great number of families in the house and in the morning a gentleman had lost his shoes. He rang the bell for his shoes. I went to see for them but could not find them anywhere in the house. I went and told him. He went quite raging mad, and told me that I had made them away. The man quite frightened me, but he could not convince my Master that I had done so. But what a kick up that man did make! Whether some of the families had taken them away in a mistake or not we could not tell.

What a variety of characters I saw at this house in families who visited it, and in their servants, and in the servants in the house! A waiter, my fellow servant, was my enemy who tattled and falsified me to Mrs. Weaver; and she at first believed him, and in her haste gave me a month's notice. But before the end of the month she found him out, and she quarrelled with him, and told him that he should leave. He said he would be d ... d if he would! and she gave him a slap on the face with her hand, and said he should. He said he would not. Then he could do nothing right for her, and it appeared I could do nothing wrong.

At the end of the month Mr. Weaver intreated me again and again to stop, but I had fully made up my mind that I would not stop any longer. Yet it was hard work for me to leave, he was so very wishful for me to stop. When on my way home I began to think I had been a great deal of trouble to my mother. I think I prayed for miles together, and as sincerely as ever I prayed in my life that God would enable me to be as great a blessing to my mother as I had been a trouble to her. (I have often thought God heard that prayer, though I was not converted.) When I got home my mother was weaving in the chamber. I went up to her. She said "What, are you come home again?" I put my hand into my pocket, and pulled out a guinea, which I gave her. Times were going hard with her, and the guinea was a timely aid; she has often mentioned it to me since.

WANDERER'S RETURN

I again began to weave, and the spare time I had I devoted it to music. Brothers Peter and Thomas had each a French horn or cornet. Our band, or say club, after purchasing the musical instruments had not much money to buy music. We bought some, and I turned author and made several marches and the band played them. We got on famously as we thought. It was called the Whitewell Bottom band.

About this time, brother Peter I and Thomas all lived with my mother and wove cotton in an outbuilding. Mr. C. Hartley of Burnley came to Whitewell Bottom for a short time, and put out cotton weft and warp to hand loom weavers, and he took a liking to brother Thomas who assisted him at times. I still thought I would get some other employment than weaving for I did not like it.

Mr. Thomas Kay of Burnley bought Longholme. I went to him and agreed with him to be a warper at fifteen shillings per week for a certain time. I had set for my work forty-eight warps per week, and what I got over I was paid the same rate as other warpers. I was very diligent and began to save money. I still continued in the band and met with them about one night in the week. Brother

Thomas wished me to get him warping. I had a promise as soon as there was a chance.

Mr. Hartley of Burnley had a mill at Feaserhouse[3] near Clithero. He wanted Brother Thomas to go to Feaserhouse and warp, and take some oversight of the concern, to which he agreed, and brother Peter took his chance at Longholme. Very shortly after, Peter came to warp with me.

Mr. Sellers (Mr. Kay's foreman) with whom we took our meat played the violoncello. But we lodged with mother who had removed to Newchurch, so that we and Mr. Sellers could any night muster up a little band of music. Altogether we were very agreeable and comfortable.

INHERITANCE

The time had come when those of us who had arrived at our majority were each to have our portion of my father's estate. Brother Thomas, Peter and I agreed that when a suitable time came we would go partners together into the cotton trade, and until such time would save what money we could.

Brother Peter and I warped together and strove like two racehorses. When I went to Longholme it was thought eight warps a day a fair day's work. Warpers at this time, when warping, sat upon a box in which was the pulley which the warper turned to turn the mill. Before the warper took his warp off the mill, he pulled the wedges out (which tightened the cord which turned the mill) in order to slacken the cord. By shifting the box and then bridling the handle of the pulley so that it could not turn round, the cord became a drag to the mill. For should the mill outrun the man who was balling the warp, the warp would slip down off the mill and would be unmanageable. In this way the warper could sit him down upon his box and take his warp off comfortably. When he had taken his warp off, he had to put in the wedges, and tighten up the cord, and make all right again.

In the time it took to do all this, another warper would warp about five bears or a quarter of warp. One day I thought I would try if I could take my warp off without slackening the cord. I thought I would ball my warp standing with my back towards the mill, and if the mill ran too fast, I could stop it with my back by bending forwards. I tried, and succeeded to my full satisfaction. I could now by this plan warp five warps in the time I had warped four, but this gave great umbrage to the old warpers. They told me I should pull down their wages. But it made no difference to me, I continued my plan. Brother Peter adopted the same plan; we were determined to get as much money as we could. We appeared very respectable and dressed like gentlemen, and saved money too.

Although I was not then a member of any church I always took care when I was in a place of worship where a collection was made, to give silver. I could not think to give copper. One Sunday I was at a charity sermon for a Sunday school; the preacher took for his text: "Thy Kingdom come." He showed so plainly to my mind how a right religious training in Sunday schools would hasten the coming kingdom of grace universally, or the millennium, that I thought while he was preaching I would give five shillings at the collection. But I thought again, if I am seen to put five shillings into the box they will think, "What in the world can be in his head, only a warper, to put five shillings into the box!" I thought, again, if I was in a public house and was to put 5 shillings down for drink, they would think it a clever thing of me. After all, I thought I would get it into the box, if I could without being seen: so when the box came, I popped five shillings under the edge of the box, and I think without being discovered.

Mr. Kay, when building some cottages at Longholme, left four cottage houses standing together without their in walls, which he fitted up for a Sunday school and preaching place for the Wesleyan Methodists. It was called Longholme Chapel. The little society agreed to send to the quarter day at Bacup three pounds per quarter to have a sermon each other Sunday morning from the itinerant preacher. When they could not raise the money, Mr. Kay lent them as much as would make up.

When I had been warping at Longholme near three years I had a very bad typhus fever brought on imprudently; I caught cold, it felt something like a sore throat, then a pain in my head and back. I thought it was nothing but what would soon go off again. I continued at my work, but my appetite continued to get worse every day. I went on in this way for about a week till I could not eat anything at all; then I went home to Newchurch, but with great difficulty. When I got home I sent for the doctor. He said I was in a very bad typhus fever. He bled me, after which I was insensible for six weeks. After the fever left me, I was so weak the doctor thought it would be almost impossible to raise me, and one time I believe he gave me up: just about the time I began to rally. I was fourteen weeks in this affliction, it was in the autumn of 1813.

When I began in this affliction I thought, if I die my soul will be lost, except God in his mercy pardon my sins. And when sensible I was in great distress of mind. I often sent for Thomas Howorth, a Wesleyan class leader, to come and pray with me, and I thought, if I should get better I would reform my life and join the church. When I got so that I could walk about, my sister Alice asked me to go to class meeting with her. I went once or twice.

While I was in the fever, I had got into my head that Mr. Kay wanted me to go into the warehouse, to assist in making up cloth and livering out work to hand loom weavers, and taking in pieces. One morning when I was raging in the fever, while my mother and family were at breakfast, I thought Mr. Kay had appointed a time, and that time had arrived, when I was to meet him for the purpose of making an agreement about going into the warehouse; whereupon I got up and dressed myself, and came down into the house. My mother said, "Whatever are you about?" I said Mr. Kay had sent for me and I was going to meet him. I got my hat and was determined to go. My mother got to the door first and stood with her back to it, and said if I went out of that house I should never come in again. She was so resolute I went and sat me down upon a chair, and in a very short time became so weak that I could not walk, and with great difficulty two of them got me upstairs to bed again.

Nothing had ever passed between Mr. Kay and me upon the subject, but when I got so well as I could go to Longholme, I went and asked Mr. Kay if he would take me into the warehouse. He said if I got strong enough and could manage the business he had no objections. I was then so weak that when hooking some 5lb. cloths, I could scarcely take them off the hooks. There were some 7lb. cloths which were to be hooked the day after, which I thought I should not be able to manage but I improved so fast in strength that I could manage the 7lb. cloth better than I had been able to do the 5lb. cloth the day before. Very soon, I got so strong and healthy that the Long Frost in 1814 had scarcely any effect at all upon me. At that time Mr. Kay sold meal and flour to his work people which we had to carry up a long flight of steps into the warehouse. I sometimes thought when I got a pack of flour weighing fourteen score upon my back it just kept me steady while walking up the steps.

I agreed with Mr. Kay for, I think, sixteen shillings per week first year, eighteen shillings per week for second year, and a guinea per week for the third year. A young man, John Clegg, one of our band, took my place for warping; he had been warping for me while I was in the fever.

We still continued to meet the band to play music about one night in the week, but did not go home to Newchurch to sleep every night, as we had done before I had the fever. I bought a bed and Mr. Sellers agreed to let us have a room to ourselves to sleep in. So we only went home on Saturday nights, remained Sunday over, and returned to Longholme on Monday morning.

Brother Thomas was still living at Feaserhouse. I was in the warehouse and brother Peter at his warping. We agreed to make some cotton pieces, and agreed for Peter to buy weft and warp, and get a few friends to weave them, and try if we could make a beginning this way. We would all keep our places and to our work until we saw how it would answer. In this way we made a quantity of cotton pieces and at a time when trade was said to be good, and goods, weft and warp, were got up very high. By the time we got our pieces made, they began to give way in price. The cotton pieces we had made cost about 26/- per piece. A spinner in the neighbourhood offered us 25/- per piece for the whole lot. But we thought it would not do for us to lose a 1/- per piece by them, so we sent them to Manchester to be sold by commission; but when we got them there they would not sell for more than 24/- per piece. We thought we would keep them until the market improved again; after a while we wrote to know what could be got for our pieces, the reply was 19/- per piece and not more. We thought it would not do to sell them yet. In a short time we heard there was more business doing so we wrote again to know how much they would sell for, the reply was then about 17/- per piece. We thought then we could not tell what to do but we came to the conclusion that they should be sold at the best price they would fetch, and accordingly gave our commission instructions. They sold them at 15/- per piece. We thought this was a bad beginning; then we agreed to wait for an opportunity.

I did not join the Wesleyan Church as I thought I would do when I was in the fever, nor did I reform my life, but grew worse. It is all of the mercy of God that I have not been ruined both body and soul. I have been in all kinds of company from the beggar to the nobility, amongst the most wicked and the most pious, amongst all kinds of labouring people and domestic servants, both good and bad. Many snares and gins have been laid for me, some of which I did but just miss, which most likely might have ruined me for ever. I often think, what a blessing that my mother had, by her example and religious training, given me in the first twelve years of my life, habits had been formed which I never could conscientiously lay aside. If I omitted divine worship wilfully on Sunday I thought some judgment would come upon me; and when I went, the preacher pointed out the wicked state of my heart so plain that I could not stand it; and then would omit going to hear preaching for a while. Then again, the habit being formed when young, I durst but go.

JOINS METHODISTS

One Sunday evening when brother Peter and I were returning home from hearing a most powerful sermon just applicable to our state, we both agreed it would not do for us to go on in the way we were going. Brother Peter began to find fault with me, he said I was too bad, I carried things too far. I said, "Well, it does not matter, I must be either one thing or another, I cannot go between. Let us at once join the Society and meet in class." He said he thought we had better. In the morning I met with James Moorehouse a Wesleyan class leader to whom I said, "You are a queer Methodist!" James said, "Come, come, David. What for?" I said, "I wonder you do not meet a class on Sunday mornings, that I could come to one." James said, "Come, David. We must mend! We must mend!" and so he left me. It was not so much that I could not meet on other nights, as I wanted to break the way; nor that I had not been invited before, but not when I was willing. In a few hours James came to me again, and, patting me on the shoulder said, "David, we have ordered a class to meet next Sunday morning." I said, "Very well, James, I am glad to hear it." He said, "You will come to it next Sunday?" I said, "Well, I'll see, James." "Nay," said he, "That will not do, we have ordered on purpose for you, you must come." I stood thinking. He said, "Come, come, David," patting me on the shoulder, "You must come." I said, "Well, James, I will come."

I turned from him, walked off; saying to myself, "Well, old Devil, it's up with thee now." I cannot express the comfort which flashed into my mind at that moment, for my decision upon a thing was almost like the law of the Medes and Persians "which altereth not." I told brother Peter what I had done and the determination I had come to, and asked him to go with me. But whatever I said, I could not prevail. He said he would see how I got on. I thought, it is a settled point with me, however; and felt no doubt upon my mind that God would accept me through His Son, although I had been so very wicked. I began to see my sins were most awful, and I wanted a full satisfaction of God's forgiving love. I met in class and continued to feel an increase of the love of God in my soul. But although I said it was up with the devil, he did not leave me, and had well nigh conquered me at one time. I got so harassed that I did not know whether God would hear my prayer or not, but I recalled praying nearly a whole day that God would influence the class leader to ask me to pray. I thought if I prayed for what I wanted the good people of God would say "Amen!" and God would perhaps hear them.

The next time I went to class, after we had sung the first time, the class leader asked me to pray. I did so, and the people said "Amen" very heartily, and my soul was abundantly blessed. I continued to meet in class and to get more love to God, and a greater sight of God's boundless love to me in the gift of His Son, who died to atone for my sins. The efficacy of His blood was so precious I felt my soul made free and could rejoice, and say and feel, "Whom Christ has made free are free indeed."

One Sunday I was at a love feast when a many, in speaking their experience, stated that they knew the day and hour where and when God set their soul at liberty and forgave them all their sins. I began to think whether I was right or not, for I could not tell the exact time when God pardoned my sins. I thought and prayed about it. The next day while at my work I resumed this subject again, but instead of reasoning with the enemy of my soul, I began to think, meditate and pray, and while doing so, a many passages of scripture came to my mind such as the following and others come now: -

And let us reason together saith the Lord; though your sins be as scarlet they shall be as white as snow; though they be red like crimson they shall be as wool. Beloved, let us love one another, for love is of God, and everyone that loveth is born of God, and knoweth God. Simon, son of Jonas, lovest thou me? Peter was grieved because he said unto him the third time, "Lovest thou Me?" and he said unto Him, "Lord, Thou knowest *all things*, Thou knowest that I *love Thee*."

I was then full of love and happy in God and said, "Lord, Thou knowest that I love Thee with all my heart and soul." I felt so confirmed that I was a child of God that I thought all the men in the world could not persuade me out of it. For I believed and felt, as I had done before, that Jesus Christ had died for me, and that He was arisen Saviour, and the Spirit itself bearing witness with mine, the spirit of adoption whereby I could cry "Abba, Father!"

I then took more to my books, reading and writing. When I had been employing myself in this way for a short time, Mr. Kay wished me to teach a set of singers for the chapel. I rather objected to it; I saw Mr. Kay was not pleased. I was fond of music but had at that time a desire to improve myself in writing and reading etc., and I knew if I taught a set of singers I should like to teach them right, and this would take up a deal of my spare time. But Mr. Kay asked me again, so I agreed to teach a set. I asked brother Peter and John Clegg to help me, who agreed. In this way we soon got a good set of singers. We took a cottage house at Longholme and then attended chapel every Sunday and sung with the singers, in the chapel. My mother came and kept house for us for a short time.

Brother Thomas was still living at Feaserhouse, and about this time he got married to Alice the daughter of John Barnes, a Methodist local preacher in the Clithero circuit. Brother Thomas joined, or rather became a member of the Wesleyan Methodist Society a short time before he was married. He and his wife came and paid us a visit at Longholme, while my mother was living with us. As soon as they came into the house my mother, in a most solemn manner, gave them her blessing. She did not live with us long because she would rather weave than keep house for us, so she returned again to Newchurch. Then sister Mary, who was a widow without any children, came to keep house for us; she was a Wesleyan Methodist. We lived very comfortably together and had family prayer in which I engaged when at home, and when away sister Mary attended to this duty.

AT BALLADENBROOK

William Clegg, who lived in the neighbourhood, had bought a ginney [spinning jenny], had taken a room, and was spinning for himself. He bought rovings, spun them into weft, and sold the weft to manufacturers. Brothers and I agreed with him, all to go co-partners, share and share alike, and each to advance an equal sum of money into the concern. Warburton had a little mill at Balladenbrook which he rented under Mr. Hargreaves of Newchurch. He agreed with us to let us have a room and turning [i.e. power, in this case a water wheel] for a carding engine. We three brothers agreed to keep our places, and for William Clegg to manage the business. We sent Clegg to Stockport as we had heard of some engines and ginneys on sale there. He went, and bought an engine and some ginneys. We had to find him all the money, as he said he had been expecting some money but had not got it.

He got the engine to work but it did its work very badly. Brother Peter and I went at nights after we had done our work, and many times stopped all night with the old engine. Brother Peter spent a great deal of time upon it, he made it somewhat better, but it did not do its work well.

One day Mr. Sharples (who was Mr. Kay's principal bookkeeper, or had some share in the concern) sent for me into the office and told me that Mr. Kay said he had been informed that I was not attentive at my work in the warehouse. I said, "Who has told him so?" Mr. Sharples, knowing that nothing less than a direct answer would do for me, said, "Your fellow warehouseman has told him." I said, "Does Mr. Kay believe him?" He said he thought he did. Then I said, "I will give you notice that I will leave your service," for I thought they would not get another man that would serve them more faithfully, nor ever do more work. And it proved so, for afterwards they had to get two in my place, for one could not do the work. My fellow warehouseman went occasionally to Burnley to assist Mr. Kay to take in cloth instead of me, and when there in order to get himself in favour with Mr. Kay, vilified me: which I believe was the greatest injury to himself for he did not afterwards stay long with Mr. Kay.

And it appeared providential to me, for I had no thoughts of leaving Mr. Kay at that time. William Clegg was managing the business very badly for us at Balladenbrook, and there was money constantly wanted for wages and waste, for it was waste we were spinning, and the weft we spun was not very well managed and was not good to sell. We were constantly at William Clegg to advance his share of money. He set one time after another to advance it, but as often disappointed us. Until one day brother Peter and I agreed that brother Peter should go and turn the hands out and lock up the room until we could come to a proper understanding. Clegg came and said he would take the place to himself. We said we would send for brother Thomas (who was still at Feaserhouse), and we would come to a proper understanding before we worked any more.

Previous to brother Thomas coming, we agreed to offer him (Clegg) thirty pounds if he would take the business and pay us the money we had advanced less the thirty pounds. He said he would take it, he would find the money in a few days, and wanted us to [de]liver him the keys, and he would set the people to work again. We said no, we would have a final settlement before any more work should be done. He said, well, he would find the money, he came again, and wanted to know if we would take a bondsman [one who becomes surety by bond]. We said we would if he was good. He named several. We said we would take one of [those] whom he had named, or we would take his uncle Clegg.

When brother Thomas came, William Clegg asked us how much we would give him to take the business to ourselves. He brought nothing into the concern except his ginney, worth about three pounds. We agreed to give him eighteen shillings per week for the time he had been in business with us, and six pounds in cash, which he accepted. And a dissolution of partnership was drawn up and signed, and we took the business to ourselves.

Brother Thomas kept his place at Feaserhouse, and brother Peter kept to his warping and looked after the business at Balladenbrook at nights after he had done his work or warping. And when my notice was up, I left Mr. Kay, and it was agreed for me to give the whole of my time to our concern at Balladenbrook. This seemed to me to be the most momentous engagement I had ever entered into in my life. It appeared as if the whole history of my life darted into my mind at once.

I have seen servants who have advised their fellow servants holding higher stations to do what they knew to be wrong against their masters, in order to get their masters to discharge them, intending thereby to get their place. I knew one servant, a Wesleyan Methodist – his master was also a Methodist – through the badness of trade had as others had done, reduced his wage, who said to me he would not pay anything more to society: his master might pay it all for him. I have known servants, and not a few, who have flattered their masters and vilified their fellow servants to their masters with a view to raise themselves in favour with their masters, not regarding the word of God – "Accuse not a servant unto his master lest he curse thee and thou be found guilty. Who art thou that judgest another man's servant: to his own master he standeth or falleth." Weavers also, pilfering their master's weft, making it very difficult for a master to get his work wrought up and brought back honestly.

I had not had a college education, but I had a schooling, and have seen as many shades of human nature as most of my age.

Such a multitude of circumstances coming like a flood into my mind at this time, it felt to me like a substance, a most ponderous thing. I was walking: I looked up; the mountains seemed high and bold, and I less than ever. I prayed; my prayer was, as near as I can tell, "Lord God, Thou hast made the hills and valleys. Thou God of the heavens and earth, teach and direct me in this undertaking. I see without Thy help I cannot manage it. Lord, be my God and my Guide; for the sake of Christ, hear me, O God." This was the substance of my prayer at this time.

THOMAS WHITHEAD & BROTHERS

My brothers and I agreed that the firm should be called Thomas Whitehead and Brothers, and that we would never draw any accommodation bills, nor allow other Houses to draw bills upon us, except foreign bills of exchange on account of foreign goods or produce shipped to us from such foreign ports. Brother Peter attended to his warping and at nights assisted me in planning. He was very diligent and persevering.

We had not been brought up mechanics but had good ideas of mechanism and we soon made a great improvement in our machinery. Balladenbrook was little more than half a mile from Longholme, so sister Mary, brother Peter and I still lived together at Longholme, so that brother and I had the opportunity of planning or advising with each other every night.

We had got a large stock of weft on hand which did not sell well. I bought some warps and began to manufacture. I got a few weavers in the neighbourhood of Balladenbrook. I got my mother who lived at Newchurch to weave for us, and a few weavers more at Newchurch. I took in pieces at my mother's house, and made them up there, ready for the market. My mother was one of the best weavers I had, and when I had any cloths more difficult than the rest, I gave them to her to weave. And, what is worth remarking, when she was sixty years old, she wove us six pieces per week for

Thomas Whitehead.

which I paid her two shillings and sixpence per piece. I believe her cloth was the best cloth as regards workmanship of any weavers we had.

Balladenbrook was a small place and had no shop to sell any food. The workpeople complained of having so far to go to buy their food. So I began to sell meal and flour, and other grocery.

We soon found that it was an advantage to us to have no other partner. Everyone seemed to have more confidence in us than when we had another partner. I alluded to something of this kind to a spinner with whom we were doing some business. He said, "Your father was a good, honest man. I knew him long before you, and we have no fear of you." I often thought that my father, being well known and had a good character was worth more to us by ten times than all the money he left us: the benefit of a father with a good character cannot be valued.

Warbourton, who had the mill of whom we took the room, had a woollen engine and carded woollen for country people. His business was not doing well for him. He said if we had no objections he would [de]liver up the mill to us. We went with him to Mr. Hargreaves, of whom he rented the mill, but did not agree with Mr. Hargreaves about the mill at that time. We found with all the money we could collect together we had little enough. We got mother to go and see if she could prevail of old Mr. Thomas Hoyle of Manchester [the calico printer mentioned above] to lend us a hundred pounds. My grandfather Lionel Blakey was one of the "Friends" (called Quakers) as was also Thomas Hoyle. They were relations and fellow play boys. My grandfather Blakey died when my mother was very young so she hopt [hopped, i.e., came out of the sect] her mother not being of the Quakers.

She went to Manchester to see Thomas Hoyle and told him what we wanted. He was very glad to hear her, for see her he could not, for he was gone blind; I know no reason why except old age. He said to my mother, "What, I suppose thou wants thy sons to get on and do well in the world?" My mother said she

Peter Whitehead.

should like us to do well and live to God. He said, "Well, I will think about it."

My mother remained there all night, and after inquiring more about us he said, "I will think about it and thou must tell David to come, and I will talk with him." He said, "How art thou going home?" My mother said, "I intend to walk." He said, "No! Thou must ride home, and I will pay the coach fare. But I will not give thee the money. If I did thou wouldst most likely put it into thy pocket and walk; but I will send George with thee to the coach office and he shall pay the coach fare. Then I shall know that thou wilt ride!"

On Monday I went to Manchester see Mr. Thomas Hoyle. (I stopped all night at his house, and attended Manchester market on the Tuesday). He made particular inquiry of me, what we were doing and what we intended to do. I answered every question (which were not a few), as positively as I could. He told me how he began business. He said "I was born at Fallbarn near Rawtenstall, and when I came to Manchester I had about fifty pounds. I began to keep shop. It did not answer for me. I continued till I had lost about all my money, then I got to be a journeyman dyer. My wife spun Jersey or woollen yarn; she generally spun all night on Friday nights in order to give time for cleaning up on Saturdays. She kept us both. I saved my wages until I was able to set up dyeing on my own account."

His conversation was very encouraging and instructive to me. I mentioned the sum of money we wanted to borrow of him. He said, "Our Lord says: From him that would borrow of thee, turn not thou away. I have been thinking about it and who knows but I may make thee ride in thy carriage? I have made some ride in their carriages by helping them into business. I will lend thee and thy brothers one hundred pounds but thou must take care to pay me the interest punctually, and thou must come and stop all night with me when thou comes to the market, and then thou canst tell me how you are getting on."

I went to Manchester market about once in a fortnight or three weeks. I generally walked to Manchester on the Monday afternoon and stopped all night with Mr. Thomas Hoyle who always inquired after our business and my mother and brother and sisters; and he told me many anecdotes.

One time I went, and after his usual inquiry I told him that my sister Betty had got married and lived at Newchurch. He asked me whereabouts in Newchurch? I said, "The next door to Samuel Lord, the butcher." He said, "I once knew a butcher who lived there called Peter, and I knew a church parson who lived at Newchurch at the same time. He was fond of his glass and good living, and had outlived his income and was much in debt. One Sunday morning he ordered his servant man to go and get a joint of meat for dinner of Peter. His servant man went to Peter for a joint of meat but Peter told him his Master must have no more till he had paid for the old. Through this, and other things he had to do, the servant was too late to church. His Master had finished prayers and was preaching. Just as he was coming into the church, his Master was saying, "And what said Peter?" He looked up at his Master and said, "He said you must have no more till you have paid for the old."

He told me this anecdote well, and more than once, and I as often responded to it as though I had not heard it before. He had been a sound business man and had a good memory of things done in his younger days and his conversation generally was profitable.

BETTY WOOD

Sometimes it happened that I had not time to stop all night with Mr. Thomas Hoyle. One Tuesday he sent his servant man George to the warehouse which I attended, to inquire for me. George said "I think you had better come and stop all night once in three weeks or a month at least, as it will satisfy my Master better. He would not be content without me coming down to see you today." I said "I will take care to do so." He liked to have a chat with me. One time he said, "David, how old art thou?" I said "Twenty-seven years." He said, "I think thou had better get married, it is better for young men in business to have a wife. Thou art old enough; hast thou seen a woman that will suit thee?"

This was a question which I did not like to answer. But I knew I could not satisfy him with less than a positive answer. Therefore, I said, "Yes, I have." This give rise to many more questions such as, "Whose daughter is she? Where does she live? Is she of the same religion as thyself? Has her father any money?"

I said "She is the daughter of Jonathan Wood who lives in the township of Bradford near Clithero. She is of the same religion as myself. Her father is a farmer and I think in good circumstances." He said, "Thou must ask him how much money he will give thee with her." I made no reply, for I thought I should do nothing of the kind. He said, "How did thou meet with her?" "I met her when I was seeking waste in that country." He asked me a-many other questions, some of which I could not answer.

When I came again, Martha, his housekeeper who was a very nice woman, said, "David, thou must not give an answer to all his questions but put him off as well as thou can, for he tells all again to me." He generally asked me how soon I intended to be married and said that when we had fixed the day I must let him know and he would keep up the wedding day. I promised to let him know when we had fixed the day, so accordingly I did. He said, after we were married I must bring my wife; "I cannot see her but I can feel her and hear her, so thou must be sure to bring her." I told him I should be very glad to do so, and would not forget.

I met with my wife in the following way. I heard that there were some mills about Hurst Green and Ribchester, and also a little mill at Twiston near Pendle Hill, and that there was some good waste to sell at these mills, which I thought I would try to buy. In this tour I had the first interview with my wife. A considerable time before this, once when brother Thomas was on a visit from Feaserhouse to us, I asked him if he knew any young woman in his neighbourhood who would suit me for a wife. He said, "I cannot tell, but there is a farmer, Jonathan Wood, who has a daughter who is a very decent and religious woman; but whether she will suit thee or not I cannot tell. I thought, she is no worse for being religious. For I had thought for a long time that if ever I did marry, I should like to have a pious woman for my wife. And though it may seem strange to some people, I had for years before I was converted gone into sacred places wholly on purpose to pray that if ever I had a wife, she might be a pious woman. I always thought it would be such a thing to have a wife who could not train up her children; should she have any, in a religious way. The idea of having a woman without religion for my wife, when I was serious, appeared to me a most awful thing. But at the time I mentioned this, I had very little thought about marrying anyone. But when I used to write to [my] brother I would ask him in a joking way how that young woman of mine was coming on? At the same time, I did not think much about it. Nor perhaps did he, for he never said anything to her about it. Brother Peter went over to see brother Thomas. He told me when he came back that he had seen Miss Wood and had had the pleasure of taking tea with her. She was cousin to brother Thomas's wife. Peter said he did not know whether he would let me have her or not, as we were accustomed to trot [tease] one another a little. Nothing more was thought. After this tea party Miss Wood's associates told her that she should have Peter. "Nay", she said "I'll not have Peter. There is another, called David. I'll have him when he comes."

When I took my tour before alluded to, in search of waste, I told brother Peter I should be within a few miles of Feaserhouse and I would call upon brother Thomas, and might I perhaps stop a few days with him. Brother Peter said, "Well but don't say anything to Miss Wood." I said, "Hast thou made her an offer?" He said, "No, I have not." I said, "Art thou intending to?" He gave me to understand that that was another thing, and said I must not say anything to her. I said, "If thou intends to make her an offer, I will promise thee that I will make no offer or say anything to her in that way. But without a positive answer from thee, I will be at liberty to do as I think proper."

He laughed heartily, but I could get no answer. I went on the Saturday and arrived at brother Thomas's house in the afternoon. It happened that Miss Wood had intended to go see her sister on some business, instead of which she sent her cousin George. His way being past brother Thomas's house, George called. When he returned he said, "Thomas's brother David is come. He has a fine red face!" Miss Wood said, "Well, father, I should have gone as I had intended; I am always in the fields when I should be in the lane." Her father said, "Well, maybe you may have a chance yet."

Up to this time Miss Wood had not any knowledge that I had ever said anything about her, nor had I any knowledge that she had ever said anything about me. On Sunday brother Thomas, his wife, and I went to Bradford Chapel. Mr. Wood's house was on our way. We called, as I think brother Thomas and his wife often did. It was a thatched house, although a farm house. It was very clean about the house, and the windows particularly so. I thought, there are some clean people here and no mistake. We went forward to chapel and also Mr. Wood's family. It was their love feast, in which I spoke, and I had an opportunity of hearing Miss Wood speak.

On our return from chapel we called at Mr. Wood's again. Miss Wood asked us to stop to tea as there would be only a little time before preaching in the evening. Brother Thomas rather objected, and said he thought it would be rather intruding upon them, having taken tea with them only the Sunday but one before. I thought I should like to stop, but thought if I did not speak brother Thomas would block up the way. I said, "Well, brother I think I have had an invitation and I shall accept it." This settled the matter and we had a very comfortable tea, and I had a very pleasant conversation with Mr. Wood, and I felt quite at home with all the family. The next day I went to Hurst Green and Ribchester to look after waste, and returned in the afternoon to my brother's. On my way to Ribchester and back, I could not get Miss Wood out of my mind. For I thought, from the first sight of her, she was just the person for me – if I should suit her. I made up my mind that if I could get an interview with her that evening I would make her an offer. I meditated and prayed about it on my way nearly all the day walking from thirty to forty miles: that if it was right in the sight of God for me to have her for my wife, that it might be so ordered that I might be able to have an interview with her that evening. And if He saw it not good for me to have her for my wife that all my attempts might be frustrated.

I tried according as I had been praying to have an interview with her, and succeeded. I made her an offer; she told me she was too young to take any step like that at present. I said time would remedy that, and as she perhaps had not much knowledge of me or our family, I would leave the matter with her for a month. In the meantime I would write, and after mature consideration and inquiry I hoped that she would reply. This was the purport of our conversation, as I had only about fifteen to twenty minutes private conversation with her at this time.

Her father, Jonathan Wood, of Dovesyke, West Bradford, Yorkshire, was for many years a useful Class Leader and the principal stay of Methodism in that place. He was brought to God in the year 1789 or 1790, when Methodism was first introduced into Bradford by one of the preachers who was then travelling in the Colne circuit.

On one occasion, it is believed the first time William Bramwell preached in a farm house in the neighbourhood when Mr. Wood and his wife heard him. At the conclusion of his sermon he requested that anyone who felt inclined to give their hearts to God to remain after the congregation had dispersed, when he proposed to form a class; and he inquired who were willing to give their names. Mr. Wood and Betty his wife were the first to come forward and have their names placed on a Methodist Class Book. The Word of God in that place grew, and believers were multiplied till the large room in the farm house was too small, and a chapel was projected and later erected at Bradford. In which Mr. Wood took a lively interest and assisted all he could, not only by giving of his substance, but his time; and lending his cart and horse to fetch materials for the building. He was a Trustee and a Circuit Steward and his house was for many years the home of the preachers when on that part of the circuit. It was always open to entertain strangers, so much so that it became proverbial and was styled "The Pilgrim's Inn." His children were watched over with great care and always taken to all the means of grace. He had the satisfaction of seeing his two only daughters brought to God when very young and become members of his own Class and of the Church of God.

[Here follow some eleven letters between David and Betty Whitehead, reproduced at the end of this volume.]

I went on Monday night to see my intended wife according to arrangement. I had, as Miss Wood stated in her letter, soon after our acquaintance urged our being married on account of the shop at Balladenbrook, and had not said anything to the contrary. Our business had increased so much that I wanted some help. We agreed for brother Thomas to leave Feaserhouse and come and help me. The last time I visited Miss Wood before the above alluded to, my brother Thomas was about to remove in a few days. On my return home, he accompanied me part way on the road, and I then told him I thought he had better take the shop. But when I was with Miss Wood, I thought more about being married than business, and I did not tell her anything that I thought about the shop. Nor did I think it was of any consequence for we had not said anything about the shop for some time. But Miss Wood had mentioned it to her people as one reason why I was so urgent to get married.

Her Uncle Joseph brought brother Thomas's goods in his cart to Balladen. When he returned home he met Miss Wood's father who made some inquiry about me. And he told him things, no doubt just as he had understood, or what he might infer from what brother Thomas or I might have said to him. We thought he had no knowledge of my connections with Miss Wood. Nor did we say anything to let him into the secret, so, many things he told Mr. Wood might be his own inference. Mr. Wood, not having much acquaintance with us nor our way of doing business he thought there was something very strange in this affair and when he came home, he talked very keenly to his daughter, which led to the two unpleasant letters. After an explanation, we were all very sorry that there had been any misunderstanding. But all was made right and the marriage was to be according to the arrangement.

I was married to Miss Wood July 7th 1818. After we had had our marriage week, my wife and I went to see Mr. Thomas Hoyle of Manchester, according to my promise. Martha his housekeeper was the first to receive us into his house; to whom I introduced my wife. She said, "Well, David, this is some nice waste thou hast found!" reminding me of my tour after waste when I first met with my wife. Mr. Hoyle was highly pleased that we had come to see him; we remained with him a few days. He told us he kept up the wedding day on the day we were married. My wife was well pleased with our visit, they were so very friendly and homely. I continued my visits with him, occasionally as before.

I had taken a house at Balladenbrook and furnished it at a very little expense for I wanted all the money I could spare for the business. My wife was a most excellent cook and had a good knowledge of domestic economy. We were both of one mind as regards economy; she kept an account of the cost of the house, and when we looked up what the house cost, we found it to be only about ten shillings and sixpence per week. Our food was very good, but there was no waste, it was so well and neatly cooked. She soon convinced me that I had made a great mistake in my letter to her, when I said I was as well attended-on as perhaps I ever should be. I had then little knowledge of a wife's care and attention.

My Class Leader, James Moorehouse, asked me to begin a Class at Balladenbrook. So, according to his desire, I began a Class which consisted of my wife and I, and brother Thomas and his wife. James Moorehouse appeared to be the Bishop of Longholme however, he gave me a Class paper and made me the leader of the Class. Shortly after, we got a few more workpeople (who were Methodists) who came to my Class; one of whom was John Hartley, a local preacher. So I got John Hartley to lead my Class. He often asked me to lead it myself, but I prevailed of him to go on leading the Class, for I thought him better qualified than I for that office.

EXPANSION OF THE MILL ENTERPRISE

After we had made an agreement for the mill with Mr. Hargreaves for a term of seven years, he also agreed to build us a spinning shop, and we got a new weft engine upon the most improved plan, on which we carded Bengal cotton, and turned off 1,000 1b. per week and sometimes more. I heard of a small farm to let at Hall Hill near the Mill. It belonged to Dr. Haworth of London. Mr. Hargreaves, of whom we took the mill, was his steward. My wife went to ask her father to come over and look at the farm and give me his opinion. He came, and after surveying it, he went with me to Mr. Hargreaves, of whom I took the farm for a term of seven years. My father-in-law was very glad that we had now got a farm. I believe he thought more highly of the farm than our mill. He gave me money to stock the farm, so after living about eleven months in the cottage, we removed to Hall Hill.

The new improved engine did its work so well, we got another of the same kind; and the old engine which we had had for a companion all night so often, we now turned adrift. Brother Peter spent many nights upon it; we spent more time and money upon that engine than would have paid for one of the new ones. But we learned a good deal by it. Brother Peter and I did not like to give up anything, and a more persevering man than Brother Peter I never met with in all my life, he certainly did make it do its work in the end. But it did very little in comparison to the new ones. It was, as the parson said to the steward of the sick club when they asked him what he would charge them for a sermon — he said, "A guinea." They told him they had had one preached for ten shillings. "Well," he said, "I could preach you one for ten shillings, but then, it would not be fit to be heard!" And I am sure the old engine was not worth its room.

Our business continued to increase, and we took care to be punctual in all our engagements and never to break a promise of payment. Once I made a promise to pay a sum of money at a certain time, and when the time fixed came within ten days or a fortnight, I could not tell where or how I must get the sum of money I had promised. I went to the Lord and told Him all about it, and prayed that He would open a way for me. Day after day passed away, and I could see no way how to meet my engagement. I tried to sell something, but every way seemed to be blocked up. I went to God again and again, and asked Him to make a way for me so that I might not break my word. A few days before the time, I was walking on the road when to my amazement a woman came out of her house, ran across the road to me and said, "David, I have a sum of money which I want you to take at interest for a while." It was exactly the same amount I had promised. "Well, I said, I will take it if you will engage to give me a fortnight's notice before you want it back again." She said she would do so and gave me the money. It was more surprising to me because I could not have thought of going to the same person for any favour of that kind.

I thought, I must take care that I do not push business too fast. When I began business I had no thought of getting rich, but a desire to do the best I could in my business, not to overrun it nor neglect it, and after that to leave the event to providence, and be thankful for whatever it might be. My greatest pleasure was to manage my business in the best way. When we began business in 1817, trade was very bad; so much so that some of our friends who knew we had saved a little money (and no doubt they were afraid we were going to lose it all) said to us, "There will never be a good trade in the cotton again, it is quite overdone." Some said there were goods enough made to fill the sea. They said, "You must not think to do as Mr. Thomas Kay and Mrs. Charles Hartley, and other manufacturers of Burnley have done, those times are all gone by." I said little to them but I thought, I understand the business, and I am not afraid to work; and it will be bad indeed if I cannot get as much or more than any wages any other manufacturer can afford to pay me. If I can do that I shall be satisfied, for it is the business I have intended to pursue all my life up, and it is my pleasure to be in this business. These clouds of darkness had now passed away and we had now a good trade. I took in pieces at Haslingden one day in the week, and also one day at Newchurch and one day at Balladenbrook. For some time brother Peter, when he had done his warping at Longholme joined brother Thomas and I every Friday night, and we hooked up all the pieces, loaded the cart, and sent them off to Manchester. Sometimes it was as far as four o'clock on a Saturday morning before we had done; and for perhaps twelve months or more we generally received a letter back per cart on Saturday night, that the goods were sold.

We bought cotton and employed a spinner near Todmorden, Mr. Bottomley, to spin weft for us on commission; and another spinner at Burnley to spin twist for us on commission. We also took a mill at Bridgend near Newchurch in which we got six throstles and one weft engine. When we took this mill brother Peter left Longholme and went to manage the mill. He understood how to manage it well.

Soon after, he joined the Wesleyan Methodist Society. Mr. John Farrar was then in Bacup circuit and I got him to come and preach at my house Hall Hill. He always stopped all night with me when he came. Although Mr. John Farrar had some odd sayings, yet he was a favourite of mine. I got much good under his ministry. He could preach more gospel in fifteen minutes than some preachers could preach in fifteen sermons.

One time, when at my house he said, "David, how did you begin your business at Balladenbrook?" I said, "We got one engine at first, and after a while we got two." "Well, and what have you at the other mill at Bridgend?" I said, "We have one weft engine and four throstles and we intend to have two more throstles." He said, "David", stroking up his forehead with his hand, "Discontent is a work of the devil!" A short time after, I was passing through Rawtenstall, and Mr. Farrar was just going to preach in a house in Rawtenstall. I thought, I will stop and hear Mr. Farrar. When I got into the house they were singing. Mr. Farrar stood in one corner and I stood in the middle of the room. He took his text and divided it: one head was, "Discontent is the work of the devil." After showing (upon this head) a number of ways how people were discontented in their present state some wanting to have as fine a house as their neighbour or to be as rich, have as fine a dress or as pretty a cloak etc. discontent is a work of the devil. Then he said, "Man gets a little mill and one engine. Discontented, he wants two, discontented he gets another mill and four throstles. Discontented he wants another two. Discontent is a work of the devil! etc."

I stood within about three yards of him looking him right in the face; he stroked his chin and his forehead, and dashed away in good style. It was a good sermon and I thought, those whom the cap would fit might put it on. But it has always been my idea that the greater the improvement in machinery or any other science, rightly appreciated, then the greater good to all human beings, and all animal creation. And whoever may have the money or the fine houses, let me have the pleasure of improving machinery, commerce and political economy. For there must be a great change in all these things before the millennium.

METHODIST CLASS LEADER

One day when Mr. Farrar came to my house (I had to renew tickets for my Class that night), I told him that my name was the first in the

Class book as the Leader, but John Hartley was the Class Leader. He made no reply to me, so I thought he would alter my name and put John Hartley in its place, and appoint him the Leader. When the tickets were renewed, I was spoken to as the Leader of the Class. But I had got John Hartley to lead the Class, and it felt to me not right to be addressed as the Leader. When Mr. Farrar gave the tickets to the Class that night, he addressed me as the Leader of the Class, and at the conclusion prayed for me as the Leader.

I thought this was very strange and I felt it very keenly – I had so very often refused to lead the Class when John Hartley had asked me so that John had not asked me for some time. It continued to be such a pressure upon my mind that I was called the Leader of the Class and did not lead it, until I became very uneasy but did not mention it to anybody but Mr. Farrar. He made no reply, nor seemed to take any notice of me. One day, when meditating about it to satisfy my mind, I came to this conclusion: that I would concern myself no more about it, but if John Hartley should ever ask me again, I would try. So my mind was then quite at ease.

In a short time after, I think the same week, John Hartley came to me and said, "David, you must lead the Class tonight." I was speechless before John, for I was at once reminded of the conclusion I had come to in my mind and could not tell what to say to John. I went to the Class at night; John Hartley did not come and the time was up, so I gave out a hymn, and just when we were concluding singing, two local preachers came in. After I had prayed and told my experience, I thought, I must first speak to these local preachers. I did so, and we had a good meeting. I could not get John Hartley to lead the Class anymore. I thought I was not qualified for the office, but I must do my best. But just at the time, there broke out a revival of the work of God amongst our workpeople at Balladenbrook, and the Class soon numbered up to about forty members. In this revival it was not hard work leading the Class. It was not a noisy revival, but a melting, softening, yielding up to the power of God. It was a lovely Class.

RAWTENSTALL HIGHER MILL, 1822-24

I continued to visit old Mr. Thomas Hoyle as usual and he made his usual inquiries, such as how many cows or horses I kept on the farm; so I had to tell him every advancement I made [such as] when I bought a horse and began to ride to Manchester Market. After some time I bought a gig in which another gentleman used to accompany me to Manchester Market. So when I bought the gig, amongst the rest of his inquiries, I had to tell him. He seemed pleased that I was now able to ride to the Market in my own carriage. Martha, his housekeeper, again told me that I should not tell him everything he might ask me for, she said, "He tells his friends who call upon him that now thou art able to ride in thy own carriage."

I believe he took a great interest in our prosperity, and was well satisfied that he had lent us the one hundred pounds; for before his death, he ordered the one hundred pounds to be divided amongst us in the following way, viz: my mother and I, brother Peter and Thomas, each to have twenty pounds; sister Alice and sister Betty each to have ten pounds; which was divided and paid to each as above. He was a good friend to us both with his money and advice.

I had been making great improvements upon the farm, such as draining, liming, etc. Doctor Haworth of London, my landlord, came to look over his estates, along with his steward, Mr. Hoyle of Haslingden, whom he had made his steward instead of Mr. Hargreaves; the reason of his change I never knew. When Doctor Haworth went over my farm he was wonderfully pleased; he told the steward that I was the best farmer by far, and, if I had a mind, he would grant me a lease for fourteen years, and he should like me to have it my life. He came over again in a few days, so I told him I would take the land on a lease for fourteen years if he would lay sixty loads of lime upon the farm per year, and I would also lay 60 loads of lime on the farm per year, to the end of the lease. He said he would lay thirty loads on, and I must lay sixty loads on. I wished him to say sixty loads, but he would not agree to that.

In the morning I thought I would go over to Haslingden and take his offer, but when I got there the steward told me he was gone to London, and he was not quite suited that I did not take his offer. I said "Well, you must write to him and tell him that I will take his offer." He did so, and Doctor Haworth gave him authority to grant me a lease. So I told the steward that I would have a proper lease. He said, well, I might please myself, but he would not be at any expense. I said, "Well, I will pay that myself." So I got a proper lease drawn up and Mr. Hoyle signed it for Doctor Haworth.

Thanks be to God, under his providence our business had prospered in our hands, so that in 1822 we bought an estate of land of Doctor Law of Newchurch, for which we gave £999, on which we built our Higher Mill at Rawtenstall and we commenced working it in 1824.

LONGHOLME CHAPEL, 1826

While building this mill, there was a great deal said about enlarging the chapel at Longholme, or building a new one. In a conversation, Mr. Thomas Kay stated that he had always thought the Longholme Chapel was built in the wrong place. In his opinion, Rawtenstall was the most proper place, it being the most central. There was not much interest, then, but he would any day give thirty guineas towards a new chapel there, and convert the Longholme Chapel for his own use. Mr. Davis, who was stationed in the Bacup Circuit made himself very busy about the Longholme Chapel. He also brought it before the quarter-day at Bacup, and laid his plan before the meeting. Which was to put a gallery into the Longholme Chapel, which chapel was Mr. Thomas Kay's private property. Therefore, his plan was to have Trustees, which Trustees should take the chapel at a rent from Mr. Thomas Kay, and be responsible to Mr. Kay for the rent. For, he said, the time had not yet arrived for a new chapel, and that subscriptions should be made for the alteration. When the time should arrive for a new chapel, the Trustees should be at liberty to remove the gallery and such things as they had put into the chapel.

He wanted me and my brothers to be Trustees along with some others. I said I thought it would be much better to build a new chapel than make the alteration he had mentioned: for which I should have no objection to be a Trustee. But I would not be a Trustee for the chapel on the plan he had proposed. He said there could not be money raised to build a new chapel. I said I thought there could; on which he differed very much from me, and said many hard things for objecting to be a Trustee on his plan. I told the quarter-day meeting, if they adopted Mr. Davis' plan, I would make no objections further than I would not be a Trustee. But I would give them something towards it, and I would take a pew in the chapel. I was certain if they adopted that plan they would make a great mistake, but nothing was settled that quarter-day.

My brothers were of the same opinion, and would not be Trustees on Mr. Davis' plan. As the alteration of the chapel was much talked about in the course of the quarter, we thought most likely it would be brought forward again at the next quarter-day. We felt a delicacy in stating that we would give towards the erection of a new chapel before Mr. Thomas Kay, Mr. Earnshaw and Mr. Dawson had stated what they would give. But we came to this conclusion, that we could not be clear if we did not tell them before anything was finally settled, what we would give towards the erection of a new chapel.

Therefore we sounded our workpeople and Balladen Class to know what they would give towards the erection of a new chapel. After which my brothers and I concluded to make up what they would give, into three hundred pounds, if a new one was erected. As I had been so hardly dealt with at the last quarter-day, I did not like to go to the next, so we agreed to send the following letter to the Circuit Stewards, and a copy of the same to Mr. Thomas Kay.

March 24th, 1824.
Messrs. Earnshaw and Dawson,

Gentlemen,
Having looked over and more fully considered the proposed plan of alteration in the Longholme Chapel, and its counter-push which proposes the erection of a new chapel, we feel inclined to think that a new chapel will be much better.

First, because the alteration at the commencement of the lease and the proposed alteration at the termination of the lease, will be, considerable waste of money. Second, because there will be no suitable burial ground. Third, because we think by unison of effect of all that are interested therein, a chapel might be erected with great advantage to the place itself and the circuit at large.

And when we first made mention of a new chapel to Mr. Kay or Mr. Davis, we thought none other than this being the case, if you should think proper to accede to this, (we sincerely hope you will), we will take upon us to raise the sum of three hundred pounds towards erecting a chapel including our own work people and Balladen Class.

From Yours respectfully,
Thomas Whitehead and Brothers.

P.S. We have sent a copy of this letter to Mr. Thomas Kay, and thought proper to send one to you also. As tomorrow is the quarter day, we thought when you were all together, you might determine upon the subject. Please to give our respects to Mr. Davis, and let him see the letter.

My brother John, who had been a Class Leader I think for more than thirty years, said he was very sorry that I was not at the quarter-day; for he thought if I had been there, Mr. Davis would not have said so much as he did say. He said the letter was not Methodistical, and a many other bad things about it and me. My brother John said he had never heard any man so badly called in a quarter-day before. But there was nothing done at this quarter-day as regards the alteration or erection of a new chapel. Another meeting was called and it was agreed for Mr. Davis and I to try to get some land to build a chapel upon.

Mr. Davis wrote to me on the 10th April, 1824, saying that he would meet me at Mr. Law's about two o'clock on Monday afternoon. I met him at the time. He told me of a small plot of land at Newhallhey Bridge, which belonged to Mr. Butterworth of Sunnyside. I went with Mr. Davis to see if he would sell it to build a chapel upon, but Mr. Butterworth was not at home. Mr. Law had asked us to take tea with them after we had been at Sunnyside.

On our return back I met with brother Peter I told him what we had been about. He said that was not the proper place to build the chapel, and if it was built there he would give nothing towards it. He said Mr. Kay had land at Rawtenstall Toll bar, which is the most suitable place, and that Mr. Kay had given it as his opinion that Rawtenstall was the most central place for a chapel.

When I got back to Mr. Law's, I told Mr. Davis what brother Peter said. "Well then" Mr. Davis said he would give it up. I said, "So much has been said about it that I would, if my brothers were willing, agree for it to be built at Newhallhey Bridge, sooner than not have a new chapel."

Mr. Davis came to me afterwards and gave me to understand that they would go on to build the chapel at Newhallhey Bridge if they could get the land, and that they should have my subscription. "No," I said, "I could not give anything except my brothers did." He said, "You said at Mr. Law's you would give your money whether your brothers did or not." I said, "No, I never said that. I said if my brothers were willing I would agree."

I saw it would never do for us brothers to disagree. I believe my brother Peter was conscientious, and had the prosperity of the cause of God at heart and I am very glad he was firm, for I saw afterwards, if we had built the chapel at Newhallhey Bridge we should have made a very great mistake.

THE HALL HILL ESTATE

About this time Dr. Haworth of London of whom I took Hall Hill Farm, having departed this life, had left his estates to his wife, who sent down from London instructions to Mr. Whitlow, an attorney in Manchester to sell the estates of land belonging to Dr. Haworth. When Dr. Haworth came down from London a short time before his death, he granted leases to all his tenants, and gave them a memorandum on plain paper, which no doubt he would have stood by if he had lived. But I had taken care to have a legal lease. The attorney tried to upset my lease, but found he could not. All the estates were sold free from leases except Hall Hill estate. So much for a legal lease! When estates fall into other hands then they go by the legality of the thing.

Brothers and I purposed buying the Hall Hill estate, so I invited my father-in-law and a few other friends to come and attend the sale, and give me their opinion, which they did, and attended the sale. Before the sale commenced, the attorney asked for my lease. I had ordered Mr. King, who made and held the writings of the lease to be at the sale and bring with him an abstract of the lease, which he then handed over to the attorney, who said, "Why have you not brought the lease?" Mr. King said, "That is an abstract and the lease is made in the regular form."

So all the estates except Hall Hill estate were offered for sale free from any lease. When Hall Hill estate was put up I bid up to £1,100. They put in the reserve bid, so that estate was not sold that night. After the sale I went to the attorney and told him that I would give £1,620 for Hall Hill estate. He promised me that I should have the first chance, but he could not sell it that night. I told my father-in-law and friends the same night what I had offered, and that I had a promise to have the first chance. When I got home, I told my brothers the same.

Soon after, there was a report that Mr. Kay had bought the Hall Hill estate. I went to Manchester and called upon Mr. Whitlow the attorney, and asked him if Mr. Kay had bought the Hall Hill estate, who told me he had. I said, "Did not you tell me that I must have the first chance?" He said, "Yes, I did, and you would have had it too. But Mrs. Haworth said that as Mr. Kay had bought two other estates, she should like him to have that also." After this it was reported in the neighbourhood that Mr. Kay had bought the land over my head. Mr. Davis came to my wife, and asked her if I had not said that Mr. Kay had bought the land over my head. My wife told him she had never heard me say so. She had heard me say that I had offered £1,620 for it, and that the attorney had promised me that I must have the first chance. He sifted and examined my wife every way that he could think for a long time, to try if he could find out I had sometime said that Mr. Kay had bought the land over my head. Then he wished to know if she had not heard me say something of that kind. My wife told him she had never heard me say anything of the kind. When I came home my wife said she had had Mr. Davis, and told me how he had been examining her. He had sometimes looked as pleasant as he could be, and other times seemed not pleased. It appeared to her he did everyway he could to get her to say she had heard me say that Mr. Kay had bought the land over my head, or if she did not think that I thought he had.

One night Mr. Davis had an interview with my brothers Thomas and Peter at Rawtenstall. In the course of conversation after saying many hard things of me, he told them that I was deceiving them; that I was driving to Manchester with the whip in the hand, and kept them in the dark working at home; that I had told them that I had offered £1,620 for the land, whereas he said I had never offered more than £1,100. Brother Peter told him that he believed that I had told them the truth, and that he did not believe that I should deceive them in anything; and for what he [Mr. Davis] had said that night, he would bring a charge against him, and would have a hearing either in a Leaders' meeting, or a District meeting, so he should have a chance to prove if he could what he had said that night.

In the morning, my brothers told me. I thought, this is a vile thing, to try to set us brothers at variance one with another. The more I thought about it and the worse it appeared to me. I thought, I must prove this. I set off to Manchester immediately. I went to our Commissioner Mr. John Munn, and told him that Mr. Davis had been to my brothers and told them that I had never offered more than £1,100 for the estate on which I lived. "Now, I want you to go to Mr. Whitlow the attorney, and ask him how much I offered for the Hall Hill estate, and I said get a note from him." Mr. Munn went and made the inquiry. The attorney told him that I had offered £1,620 for the Hall Hill estate, but he would not give Mr. Munn a note, but said if my brothers or any other person would call upon him, he would satisfy them upon the subject. I said brother Peter would have a Meeting upon the subject, and I should be obliged to have him for evidence upon that point.

Mr. Munn told me afterwards that Mr. Davis had called on the attorney soon afterwards who had asked the attorney the same question who he had told Mr. Davis that Mr. Munn had been to ask that question who had been told £1,620. Mr. Davis said to the attorney "You should not have told him."

One day Mrs. Law came over to me and said, "David, I have some thing on my mind that I must tell you. It troubles me so that I cannot sleep." She said Mr. Davis called on us one evening, and stopped with us till about two or three o'clock in the morning. All this time he was trying to get me to say, that you said when you were with him at tea at our house, that you would give your money towards erecting the new chapel whether your brothers gave their money or not. I told him that you said you would try to prevail of your brothers, and if things could be made agreeable that you had no objections. He examined me and cross-examined me to get me to say that you said you would give your money whether your brothers did or not, or if I did not think you meant so by what you said. She said he wrote several papers over in different ways, wishing me to sign one. But as often as he wrote his papers, there was something in all of them that she said I could not sign to. They all came to this: that you said so, or I understood by what you said to mean so, or I thought so, or it appeared so. Between writing these papers, he was telling first one thing and then another about you and your brothers. He said you were likely to be made bankrupt; then if you had given any money towards the chapel it would be got back, for at the time you promised the money you were insolvent. He said "David Whitehead had the longer end of the string, and was riding in the gig to Manchester – and had a man to sell for him, and his brothers at home working etc., so that David Whitehead was keeping them in the dark!" He also said a great deal what Mr. Kay, Mr. Earnshaw and Mr. Dawson had said about us; whether what he said that they said were true I doubt it. These gentlemen and I never had any disagreeable words together in all this unpleasant affair. But there was shyness which I have often thought was created by Mr. Davis. Mrs Law told me all these things, and many more, which I noted down against the meeting. She said she could not rest without telling me. I asked if Mr. Law was present all the time when this conversation took place. She said "He was present all the time and heard it all." I asked her if Mr. Law would attend the meeting if I gave him an invitation, she said she was sure he would. I received the following letter from Mr. Davis:

>Bacup, 21st February, 1825.
>
>Mr. D. Whitehead.
>I can now inform Mr. David Whitehead that Mr. Newton has fixed upon Mr. Riles to hear what Mr. Thomas Kay has against him (Mr. D. W.), upon reports about Hall Hill sale. Mr. Riles has fixed the meeting for next Friday, the 25th of February; I think 6 o'clock will answer best for the parties, and that our chapel, Newchurch, will be the best place. You can invite any you may wish to be at the meeting, to attend. We shall be in the chapel at the time. Please to inform your brothers Thomas and Peter of the time and place of meeting.
>
>>Sorry to be forced to say
>>Your grieved
>>Thomas Davis.

We availed ourselves of the privilege of inviting. We wrote to all the Leaders and a many of my friends the following note:

> Mr. Newton has appointed Mr. Riles to preside at a meting which will be held at the Newchurch Methodist Chapel on Friday the 25th February at 6 o'clock in the evening to hear our case respecting the erection of a new chapel at Rawtenstall etc., and what Mr. Kay has to say against us upon reports about Hall Hill land.
> We do particularly desire that you will attend the meeting.
> From Yours respectfully,
> Thomas Whitehead and Brothers.

We thought we should like to have one preacher on our side. Brother Peter went to Mr. Davis to ask him if he might invite Mr. Pilter who was then in Rochdale Circuit. When he got to Bacup, Mr. Davis was gone to Shawforth to preach (it was a weekday service). He followed him and caught him when he was about going into the chapel, and asked him, who said he had no objections. Peter wanted a note from him to Mr. Pilter. Mr. Davis said "Give him my respects, and tell him I was just going into the chapel to preach or I would have written a note to him." Mr. John Munn could not come to the meeting so he wrote the following letter:

> Manchester, 22nd February, 1825.
>
> Mr. Peter Whitehead,
> Sir,
> I am sorry it will not be convenient for me to come over on Friday next, as we are very busy at present. When I called upon Mr. Whitlow on the 3rd of January, I asked him how much your brother David had offered for Hall Hill estate and he told me he had bid him £1,620 for it after the sale was over, and he believed he might have had it if it had not been for Mrs. Haworth.
> I remain, sir,
> Yours respectfully,
> John Munn.

Now I had got all ready for the meeting which took place on Friday 25th February, 1825. When Mr. Pilter came into the meeting

Mr. Davis said "I am glad to see you though I did not expect you." Mr. Pilter told me after the meeting that when Mr. Davis addressed him in that way, he handed him over a slip of paper on which he stated what my brother had said when he invited him to come, and wished to know if it was true. Mr. Davis wrote upon the slip of paper "It is quiet true" and returned the paper to Mr. Pilter again.

After the meeting was opened Mr. Davis brought forward the reports that were going [i.e. circulating] in the country that Mr. Kay had bought the land over my head. They occupied a great deal of time, I think near two hours, talking about reports in the country and asked me if I had not said that Mr. Kay had bought the land over my head. I said that the land was in the market a Kay had as much right to buy the land as I had. If they had any witness against me they must bring them forward. But they brought no witness against me. So after a long conversation they drew up a paper in justification of Mr. Kay, and wanted me to sign it. I told them I would sign no papers upon that subject. Mr. Davis contended hard and thought I ought to sign it. I said I make no charge against Mr. Kay and they had proved nothing against me and I should not sign any paper upon that subject. The chairman said he would sign it as chairman of the meeting. They were about to close the meeting, brother Peter stood up and said he should now bring his charges forward. Mr. Davis said there was no other case, the meeting was called for the business which they had now finished. Brother Peter said, "I have a charge against you, and it was I who wished you to call a meeting, and if I cannot be heard here — I will give notice for a District Meeting, for I will be heard!" "Well then," Mr. Davis said, "You must bring your charge forward now, and it shall be gone into tonight." So Brother Peter stood up and said "Mr. Davis told brother Thomas and I that brother David was deceiving us, and kept us in the dark, that he had said to him (Mr. Davis), that he would give his money towards the chapel whether we did or not, and afterwards denied it, and that he had told us he had offered

£1,620 for the land, and had never offered more than £1,100 for it." Brother Peter went on to show that it was a serious thing to make such statements against a brother who was a partner in business as well, whom we believe would not deceive us in anything. And he said "I told Mr. Davis that night that I would bring it before a Leaders' Meeting." He mentioned several other things which Mr. Davis had said about me. He spoke about twenty minutes.

I then handed over to the chairman the letter from Mr. John Munn to brother Peter which at once set me clear about what I had offered for the land. Mr. Davis would have pretended that commissioners would write anything. The chairman asked if Mr. Munn was a respectable man; someone in the meeting said he was a very respectable gentleman, and I think Mr. Kay gave the chairman to understand so too. Then I came forward and stated at full length what Mrs. Law had told me that Mr. Davis had said about me at their house, how he laboured to get Mrs. Law to sign a paper which she did not believe to be true; and how he vilified me in order to prejudice her mind against me so as to get her to sign this paper. When I had stated in full how he had implicated Mr. Kay, Mr. Earnshaw and Mr. Dawson, and the other things which I have before mentioned, then I asked Mr. Law, who was present at the meeting, if what I had stated as regards the conversation Mr. Davis had with Mrs. Law at his house was correct. Mr. Law said, "I was present all the time the conversation took place, and what you have stated is quite correct." "Did Mr. Davis say, when at your house, at the time when we promised the money towards the erection of a new chapel, we were insolvent?" Mr. Law said, "Yes, he did."

Then I sat down. Mr. Davis stood up and said, "I deserve a censure from this meeting." The chairman, or Mr. McKitrick said "And you shall have one!" Mr. Davis said, "As regards Mr. Kay, Mr. Earnshaw and Mr. Dawson, I will exonerate them and take all upon myself. I have done wrong and I beg Messrs. Whiteheads' pardon and if they will forgive me, I will promise them that I will never say anything against them again as long as I live."

Mr. McKitrick, who Mr. Davis had invited to the meeting, spoke strongly against the conduct of Mr. Davis, and encouraged us brothers to go on, and hoped God would prosper us. Mr. Riles, the chairman, spoke against Mr. Davis' conduct. Mr. Davis put out his hand to me and asked me to forgive him. I took hold of his hand and told him that I would forgive him. Then the meeting broke up, at a late hour. The next quarter-day after this meeting, brothers and I were particularly invited to attend the quarter-day meeting as the chapel question would be brought forward. We all attended and it was put before the meeting, whether there should be a new chapel, or the alteration, viz: the old chapel raised and a new gallery etc. A great deal was said against a new chapel, alleging its prematureness, and in vindication of the alteration, Mr. Davis was the principal speaker and little was said beside what he said. It was first put to the vote for a new chapel. Brothers and I and another Leader put up our hands. Brothers Thomas and Peter were not Leaders. Mr. Davis said none could vote but Leaders. So he put it again, and there was only my hand up, and this other Leader, who said, "I do not properly understand which way I should vote." Mr. Davis said if he did not understand it, he had better vote neither way. So Mr. Davis, put it again, and then there was only my hand up for the new chapel. He asked for a show of hands from those who were against the new chapel. Nearly the whole meeting held up their hands against the new chapel. Mr. Davis said, "Only one for a new chapel and so many against it!" He then put the alteration, when nearly the whole meeting voted for the alteration. He then asked for a show of hands from those who were against the alteration. My hand was the only hand held up. Mr. Davis said, "The alteration is unanimous except one." It was then said that the minority should act with the majority, and all be at peace together. I said I could not take any active part in the alteration, but I would throw no obstacle in their way, and should they make the alteration I would take a pew in the chapel. So the meeting ended.

My brothers were very much grieved that they should invite them to the meeting when they had no vote, and that so little regard should be paid to their feelings. Brother Peter thought he would have no more to do with them about the chapel, and that we should now attend to our business and let them act as they thought proper. But in a few days after this meeting, Mr. Davis, Mr. Earnshaw and Mr. Dawson came to Rawtenstall to us, and said that Mr. Thomas Kay had agreed to sell as much land as would be wanted for the new chapel at Rawtenstall, just beside the toll bar, the place where brother Peter had wished the chapel to be erected; and that Mr. Thomas Kay had promised a subscription of one hundred guineas; and Mr. Earnshaw and Mr. Dawson had each put down a subscription, and they were come to see how much we would subscribe. We went to consult together about it. Brother Peter had had his mind so tried by Mr. Davis' conduct that he had thought he would have nothing more to do with him, and did not like to promise them anything.

I said "Well I think as they have now agreed to build a new chapel, and at the place where we wanted it, I think we should tell them at once what we will give." We agreed to do so, and told them we would give towards the new chapel as now proposed one hundred and fifty pounds, and if they would agree to build a Sunday School under the chapel, we would give fifty pounds more towards the School.

Mr. Davis then called a special Leaders Meeting of the whole Circuit, and again put it to the meeting whether there should be a new chapel or not. He asked for a show of hands from those who were in favour for a new chapel, when the whole meeting held up their hands. So it was quite unanimous for a new chapel. I could not account for the sudden change which had taken place upon this subject in so short a time. And I would never allow myself to inquire or pry into it as I felt confident if only one hand be held up, and God on his side, he will prevail though a multitude be against him.

God's ways are not our ways. He sees not as we see. He heareth prayer. He is the Lord of Lords, King of Kings. The cattle upon a thousand hills are His and the silver and gold are his. The earth is His, and the fullness thereof. He hath made the world and all things, and us, and hath preserved us. He hath given a law to every thing He hath made. The earth, sun, moon and stars obey his laws, but man, His greatest piece of creation has broken His divine law and hath wickedly rebelled against his maker, but Glory be to God, He hath loved us and manifested His love to us in the gift of His son, who hath purchased us by his blood. We are His by redemption through faith which is the gift of God, the Holy Spirit witnessing with the blood that we are born of God. When God comes down in all His attributes and power, He can melt down a multitude of his believing children and make them rejoice in His will. Yea, He can make the wrath of man to praise Him. Glory be to His name for ever.

All things are His, our factories, machinery and business and all we have are His, and we are His, and it is our glorious privilege to serve Him in our business, yea continually to serve Him in all things, both temporal and spiritual and when we live up to our privilege we can be as happy in our business as in a prayer meeting. Fully to know our privileges in the service of God is to be happy at all times in all our business. May God teach me this happy way more fully that whether I eat or drink or whatsoever I do, I may do all with a single eye to the Glory of God. Amen.

The Lord is merciful and good to me both day and night.

TEETOTAL RESOLUTION

One night when laying alone in my bed (my wife at that time being confined of David Blakey in the year 1823) I found my knees so cold that night and that it was difficult for me when alone in bed to get them warm. I began on my bed to reflect. I thought my blood is no-good and it may be with me taking now and then a glass of brandy, wine or some other spirits. The drinking custom was very prevalent in our neighbourhood at this time. For instance, if a friend called upon me at my house, the decanter, warm and cold water, sugar and glasses were ordered upon the table, and generally I and my friend or friends would take each a glass. When I went to the Market, after dinner custom was to take a glass of spirits, and another when I took my horse from the Inn.

Soon after I began business I thought it was necessary for me to take a glass of spirits at night before going to bed, for the good of my health, as I had so much work to go through. I was thought by myself and others, a very temperate man. But, on my reflections on my bed, I could remember several firms in which the market man died the first, I thought most likely through getting into the habit of taking too many glasses, and I thought if I could not adopt some other plan than taking these glasses, I should die first too!

So I came to this determination, that I would make a complete change in my living; that I would take no ale, porter or beer to my dinner, or wine or spirits, then or at any other time, except when I met with friends or men of business which objecting to take a glass with them might cause them to think I had something against them, or [that I was] not so friendly as I used to be. This, I thought, I must manage as well as I can. I never did like to take two glasses at my Inn on market day; and which to avoid I had once, for a time, had my horse at a livery stable; at which place they did not behave well to it, so I went back again to my Inn.

I told Mr. Munn, our commission agent at Manchester, that I should like to take my horse to some stable so that I should not be obliged to dine at the Inn. He said, "Mr. Haslam of Bury always puts up at The Spread Eagle, but did not dine there." I asked if he knew the landlord. He said, "I know him very well." "Then will you go with me and introduce me to him, and ask him if he will take my horse, and if it will be properly attended to, if I do not attend or dine in the house?" Mr. Munn went with me to the landlord of The Spread Eagle and asked him the question. The landlord said that if I would bring my horse there it would be well attended to, just the same as if I had dined there. I afterwards took my horse to the Spread Eagle and the hostler took good care of it. Then I could dine at a private place or some eating house without taking anything to drink but water.

I certainly have drunk many glasses of spirits through false delicacy, but I got in a while that I could manage so as scarcely ever to take a glass with anyone. I found my body to improve in strength and health. I could walk with more ease and with less perspiration. It was a happy thought on my bed, and a good thing for me that I put it into practice. How good the Lord is to me and to all in this neighbourhood! Our privileges are great.

Now we shall have a new chapel. A Building Committee was formed and Trustees fixed upon, but neither my brothers nor I, nor Mr. Kay, were Trustees. I was informed that Mr. Davis said that neither us nor Mr. Kay should be Trustees, and that the chapel should be called Longholme Chapel though it was built at Rawtenstall. When the foundation was laid, James Moorehouse, my old Bishop, christened it "Longholme Chapel." It was of little consequence to us what the chapel was called, or who were Trustees. We thought if the chapel was built, and at the right place, all would be well.

And to be relieved from being of the Building Committee, or Trustees, just suited us at this time, for we were very busy filling our new mill with machinery and setting it to work. We commenced running the steam engine in the month of November, 1824. From this time to the end of 1825 was a trying time for us in our business. We had enemies not a few, but we had some true friends; one of whom was Mr. William Heap of Halifax, a more pious, well disposed, good man I never met with in all my life.

COTTON PRICES

In consequence of short crops, there was a good deal of speculation, and cotton got up very high, say middling cotton fifteen pence to sixteen pence per lb. But providentially we had bought a good stock of cotton which cost us on an average about 10d to 10½d per lb. And fitted us until cotton came down from the above high price, to about 13½d per lb., at which price I bought as much as would fit us a fortnight. Having as I thought made a low offer, which was at once accepted, I as suddenly thought I had made a bad job of it to buy so much, and most likely it would be lower again next week. When I came home I told my brothers what a mistake I had made in buying so much cotton. They also thought it was a bad job. But a thought just struck me at that time, viz: if cotton comes down as fast as we think it will, then goods will also come down. We had at that time a very heavy stock of pieces on hand. I said brother Peter should go to Manchester, and get Mr. Munn to sell all the pieces he could for the best price he could for ready money. Which he did and on Saturday I said, "Go again and get Mr. Munn to sell all the pieces he can for ready money. Tell him we must have the money." I went on the Tuesday following and told Mr. Munn to do the same again. Mr. Munn could not tell what to think about us as we were so determined to sell. Every day we went we had to take about sixpence per piece less than we had done before, but we continued to do so till we had sold off our stock. And when we made a stand, (which we did rather too soon) the cloth which we were making was reduced in price from the highest point, say 17/s. to 18/s. per piece down to 10/s. per piece. We have often thought through me buying cotton for a fortnight instead a week, which produced the thought that goods would come down and we would sell them off, enabled us to realise about five hundred pound more for our stock than we should have done. So that that blunder was like a rap upon the head, to sharpen one up to his true interest.

Soon after, we began to work the new mill, say [called] Rawtenstall Higher Mill. We brought a part of the machinery from Bridgend Mill to that mill and sold the rest of the machinery at Bridgend, and let the mill and brought our workpeople to Rawtenstall. About the end of the year 1825 Balladenbrook lease ended; we sold the machinery at Balladenbrook and brought the work people down to Rawtenstall Higher Mill. This mill we filled with machinery of throstles, mules and preparation for the same, and power looms.

At the end of the year 1825, I had much reason to be truly thankful to God for His providential care over us these last two years, having built the mill and a many houses, and no-one of our masons or workpeople have [having] been killed. It has been a very critical time in our business and a busy time for us. And a trying time as regards religion and faith in God. Glory be to God! He has made our business to prosper, and kept our hearts right with Him. He that trusteth in Him shall not be confounded.

POWER ROOM RIOTS

We have a very dark lookout this year [1826] as regards trade. People appear to be much dissatisfied and know not where to throw the blame. The fact is there have been short crops; speculators have taken the advantage of it, and a many of them have gone too far in it and have involved themselves by which brought upon themselves and others. And workpeople are very poor economists when trade is good, and then, when trade becomes bad, having nothing beforehand, are hard up and soon in deep poverty. They blame everything but themselves. Some politicians, not of the best kind, in order to gain political influence, fix upon some popular improvement in machinery, or any other popular thing by which they think they can gain popular influence, and take the advantage of those of too great credulity and the ignorant part of the working class, and give it out that that is the cause all their misery.

THE HIGHER MILL, RAWTENSTALL.

So this Spring they sent out their emissaries to get the ignorant part of the community to believe that power looms were the cause of all their distress. Sunday meetings were held on the tops of the hills to discuss these matters, and to persuade these ignorant people to break all the power looms. Our new chapel with a good schoolroom under it was opened April, 1826, and Sunday, April 23rd was the last day of opening of the old chapel. We had a most glorious time, large congregations, good sermons and large collections. All appeared to be joy, love and happiness. But on the Monday, the day after, what change took place.

News came that there was a riotous multitude of people who had assembled at Accrington with a determination to break the power looms. The authorities of Accrington sent to Blackburn for a troop of cavalry. But before they could reach the place the rioters had broken all the power looms in that neighbourhood, and were proceeding on the road to Blackburn when they met the cavalry. The rioters saw the cavalry before they met them, and they had filled their pockets full of stones. When the cavalry came up to the mob, the Commanding Officer made an attempt to frighten and send them home. But his orders being to go to Accrington and having no Magistrate with him, could do nothing more than make an attempt.

He drew up the cavalry and commanded them to charge, as though he was going to fire right into them. The leader of the mob said with spirit and a loud voice, "Blow away, we are ready for you!" The officer said that was real English. He did nothing more but let the mob pass on. And he marched on according to his orders, to Accrington. What a pity that such fine brave spirited men as some of those workpeople are should be duped by the emissaries of politicians who are even pleading for class legislation, what they call Protection, which is legal robbery of these same poor men. When the mob got to Blackburn they began to demolish the power looms; and before the authorities of Blackburn could get the cavalry back from Accrington, a many looms were broken.

That night a meeting was called of manufacturers and Magistrates at Burnley, to take into consideration the best means of putting a stop to the breaking of power looms which meeting I attended. The Magistrates had sent for a troop of cavalry from, I think, some part of Yorkshire, but thought they would not arrive till Tuesday night. So it was agreed and ordered by the Magistrates that William Turner, Esq., of Helmshore, and I should forthwith take a post chaise, and go to Manchester for a troop of cavalry.

We went and got a troop which arrived early next morning at Haslingden. The mob assembled again and proceeded to Helmshore. Notice was given to the cavalry. They went with all speed, but the mob succeeded in breaking the power looms there. But the cavalry made about twenty prisoners, which they brought to the "New Inn" in Haslingden. The mob assembled again and came to the Inn and broke the windows and released the prisoners, which gave the mob renewed courage and they gave notice to meet the next morning at Rawtenstall and break Thomas Whitehead & Brothers' power looms. I went early in the morning to Burnley to see if I could get some more cavalry. The troops which the Magistrates had named to us on Monday night arrived in Burnley that morning. The Magistrates sent them forward to Rawtenstall with an order to pursue the mob and make prisoners. But before I could get the cavalry to Rawtenstall, the rioters had been and broken all our power looms. My brothers had got the cavalry from Haslingden, but they did no good, but we thought harm; for they did not attempt to stop the mob or make prisoners, and the rioters said, "The soldiers are on our side!" They went on and broke Mr. Thomas Kay's power looms at Longholme.

Then they proceeded to Chatterton where they met a company of sharpshooters. The rioters began to stone them, and the soldiers fired upon the rioters, who in return continued to stone them. And another part of the rioters got into the mill and were breaking looms at the same time. But the soldiers succeeded in driving them away after killing six, and wounding a great number. But shortly after, while the soldiers were protecting another mill, part of the mob came again to Chatterton, and broke the remainder of the looms. But before they got away, the cavalry which I had got from Burnley came up and made about twenty prisoners, which they tied together with ropes and marched them off to Bury. The rioters, finding Chatterton and Ramsbottom too warm for them, they returned back and came up the Valley past Longholme to Waterbarn, and broke Mr. Ormerod's power looms and went onwards through Bacup to Old Clough and broke Messrs. Robert Munn and Co.'s power looms, and gave it out that the next morning they were all to meet the Yorkshire people at Todmorden and break the power looms of Messrs. Fielden Brothers.

The Magistrates swore in a large number of special constables, many of whom had been looking on and marking the most active leaders of the rioters. The Magistrates gave them orders to go and take them out of their beds, as many as they could of those who they had marked. They went in the dead of night and fetched out of their beds about twenty men and women who had been breaking looms or aiding and assisting, whom the Magistrates committed to Lancaster to stand their trial, and they were sent of in the same night, guarded by soldiers. In the morning the inhabitants were all in amazement, one telling another that such and such an one had been fetched out of bed in the dead of night, men and women, and men taken out of bed from their wives by the constables. It put such a terror upon the inhabitants so that the Lancashire rioters did not go to Todmorden to meet those from Yorkshire. There were a many people came to Messrs. Fielden's mills at Todmorden that morning, but as the Lancashire people did not meet them, they went away without attempting to do any damage. The rioters in Lancashire were so frightened that many of them durst not go to bed in their own houses. Some left the country; others hided them for weeks, some in one place and some in another, some in coal pits and some who few, (if anybody) could have thought they would have been guilty of such a crime.

The method of arresting them in bed and taking them away at once, put a terror upon the inhabitants, and completely put a stop to the breaking of power looms. This gave me to see the superiority of the power of special constables to that of military power in putting down mobs and riots, and for the conservation of the peace of the country.

Our power looms being broken, of course our workpeople were thrown out of work, for which we were sorry. It was not their fault, they had taken no part with the rioters. Therefore we thought it was our duty to get them into work again as soon as we could. So I went, immediately after the looms were broken, and ordered new power looms to replace those which had been broken. We had anonymous letters sent, threatening to burn our factory down.

In about three days after our power looms were broken, Lieutenant General Sir John Byng[4] came to Haslingden, and sent a request to have an interview with one of us and a few other manufacturers. I had, along with some other manufacturers, an interview with him. I was asked if we had not received anonymous letters. I said we had, and at Sir John Byng's request I showed him one. He gave us to understand that it would be impracticable for the government permanently to protect with troops or garrison every mill within this populous manufacturing district, but that it was the intention of His Majesty's government to keep an adequate military force in the principal towns in this county, so as to be ready to tend to their aid when called for, to those manufacturing establishments which may be situated in a distance in the country, or not under sufficient protection. With a view to protect those mills so situated, the government would supply with arms and ammunition the owners of those mills, in order that they may place them in the hands of confidential servants and over lookers, and thus ward off any sudden attack for a period until sufficient military aid can be procured from some neighbouring town. Those manufactures who may be disposed to avail themselves of this protection, are to apply to the Magistrates of the district, who will make a requisition to the General Officer for arms and ammunition.

Soon after this interview with Sir John Byng, I received a letter from Major Watkins of Bolton, the purport of which was that I must come over to see him immediately, for my life was in danger. Directly after I received the letter, a man came and asked me if I had got a letter from Major Watkins of Bolton. I said I had. He said the Major had sent him (fearing the letter might miss its way) to tell me that I must go over to Bolton immediately to see him. I took my horse and gig and went through Haslingden and called upon Mr. Gray, the Magistrate, who accompanied me to Major Watkins. I told the Major that I was David Whitehead whom he had sent for, and introduced to him the Magistrate, Mr. Gray. Major Watkins said, "Have you a good nerve for there is a plot laid to take your life? But you need not fear, for I will take care of you. I have all the soldiers in this district under my command. There are nightly meetings in which they are laying a plot to burn your mill down in the night, and take your life. I shall know the exact time when they have determined to do it, of which I will give you timely notice. You must have plenty of beef and other eatables, and drink, in the mill. I shall have plenty of disguised soldiers in the mill at the time, and they will want something to eat. Arms and ammunition I shall send up to the mill in the night. I will send you two men; they will be true men, whom you may allow to go out and come in any time in the night as they may wish. They will take care of you, and I shall have information of every meeting and everything that is said or done in them."

He gave me his address, where I might see him in Manchester, as he should be there nearly every night, and should be glad to see me any night. So I was at Manchester most of my time for a week or a fortnight. On the 6th of May the two men came from Bolton to my house, Hall Hill, according to the arrangement, and brought with them the following letter: -

Bolton, 6th May 1826.

Sir,

The bearers hereof are the persons selected to assist you agreeable to the arrangement made on Monday evening last. You may place the greatest confidence in them. They know their duty, and have no doubt but they will conduct themselves in that manner that will be perfectly satisfactory to you. Their names I have not mentioned, not thinking it necessary so to do.

I am, sir,
Your obedient servant,
JAMES WATKINS

The two men were very civil men who remained at my house near a fortnight. They were out a great deal of the nights, and sometimes in the day. They would not answer many questions, but they gave me to understand we bore a good character generally amongst the workpeople. I often called upon Major Watkins in Manchester, but he always cautioned me against asking any questions, as he told me he would not answer any. So I sat with him and he told me what he pleased. He said, "Their plot was to come to your mill in the night and burn it down, and take your life." He would also tell how many had met in their night meetings. I think the highest number he ever mentioned to me who met at these meetings were twenty-eight. The last time I met Major Watkins he told me the night meetings were all over. He said they wanted one in the meeting to come forward a pledge himself that he would be the man, when the time came, to cut your throat, but there were not one in the meeting who would come forward and say he would cut your throat. And as they could not come to any agreement their night meetings were given up, and the plot abandoned.

This was good news to me, for had the plot come to maturity, what a catastrophe would have taken place at Rawtenstall! Such as I think could have begot in me a dislike to the place, which I never could have overcome again. But from the first notice of this plot to its abandonment I ceased not to pray that God might confound those in the plot in all their plans and frustrate their intentions, baffle them and confuse them and bring all to nought. Fully believing that God is omniscient and omnipotent and that he would hear prayer through his Son, I laid these things before him and glory be to his name, his care has ever been over me, yea He hath blessed us all and hath made our enemies as naught, lighter than chaff. Our factory and all we have is the Lord's and he hath taken care of it. The spy system is bad – tyrants and ungodly men may employ spies, but a religious liberal man with a sound mind never will. The spy system may live in dark ages but in the enlightened ages it must die.

A short time after, Mr. Gray the Magistrate called upon me and introduced to me an officer of the cavalry, whom, he said, wished to have an interview with me. The officer in the course of conversation told me that he had had a quantity of cavalry, the men sleeping with their horses, and the horses with their saddles on, for a fortnight together all ready for a march or action any moment, and all on my account. Well, I thought, it was no pleasant thing to be experimented upon in that way!

The inhabitants began to reflect on their folly. Farmers and others, and some whom we thought from their station in life ought to have known better, told labouring men and handloom weavers, that there was no law against breaking power looms. But, finding that the county must pay for the damage done, and that they must pay each their share by a rate, they learnt a lesson by their folly, which they will not soon forget. For those who pay for their own education retain it all the better.

We had to prove at Lancaster Assizes that the power looms were riotously broken, which we did, and got damages awarded. The money was collected from the inhabitants, and was paid. In the meantime we got new looms and set them to work as fast as we could, after which we had a fair trade for some time.

METHODIST REVIVAL

This year, say Methodistical Year, William Harrison was stationed in the Bacup Circuit. He was an odd man, uncommon in his manner in praying and reading, though a mannerly and good man. He was not well treated in leaving Bacup Circuit. He was invited at the March Quarter-day Meeting to stop a second year, which he accepted. Soon after, two Leaders came to me and asked me to say whether I thought it would be better for Mr. Harrison to stop another year or leave at Conference. I said, "I will not tell you, you should have asked that question at the Quarter-day." They said they expected one of the Leaders whom it had been mentioned to, would have objected to his staying a second year, but he did not make the objection at the time. "Then," I said, "You are doing wrong to mention it now, and I can have nothing more to say about it." But they went on with their canvassing, and got a great majority against William Harrison stopping a second year, of which they acquainted him. He felt it very keenly. I always thought it was cruel treatment to the old gentleman. He was succeeded by J. Worral.

The Society in Bacup Circuit continued to increase, and we had a good Sunday School at our chapel, Longholme, Rawtenstall. We made good accommodation for all the schoolchildren in the chapel, and it was agreed by the teachers of the School and the Class Leaders, that all the schoolchildren should attend preaching in the chapel every Sunday morning and afternoon. So that all who attended school should attend divine worship twice every Sunday. It is my settled opinion that any religious society who shall teach these Sunday School children or any part of them in the time of their divine worship, are giving such children a spurious religious education. It is teaching the children to believe that something may be done better than attending on divine worship. The preaching of the Gospel is a divine appointment, and to teach the children not to attend upon it is a sin. No wonder if a many of such Sunday School children should become infidels. They are made to believe to hear the word of God is only a secondary thing, which can be left to a convenient time with a good conscience.

When talking with a gentleman of Bolton upon this subject, he told me he had a servant girl living with him who had been a Sunday scholar in a Sunday School in Bolton; which school seldom took the children to hear the Word of God preached; perhaps they would take some part of the children once on a Sunday, but had a sermon preached in the School once in a month to all the scholars. This servant girl never wanted to go to chapel to hear preaching, but would always go to this School once in a month to hear the sermon preached to the scholars. He believed if he would not allow her that privilege, she would leave her place. How true! Train up a child in the way he should go, and when he is old, he will not depart from it. This view which I took, always made me firm, that all who attended our School should attend the chapel twice every Sunday to hear the word of God preached.

Our Society increased and we now wanted a second preacher. Mr. Dawson and I being the Circuit Stewards at this time, we had to give a pledge to the Conference that in four years we would take a second married preacher; and in 1827 T. Slug and H. Fish were stationed in the Bacup Circuit.

Soon after their appointment to our Circuit a keen affliction took place in my family. My eldest son David Blakey, a little over four years old, having had the measles, which left something in his constitution which Nature, with all the help we could procure, could not throw off. He had a fine temper, great caution, often on his guard in speaking, difficult to get a promise of anything from him without "Happen!" or "Perhaps I may!" He had a strong, persevering mind; if he could not obtain the thing he wanted, he would try again and again, wait sometimes a day or two, and would try again, and if not successful, he appeared greatly disappointed. He had a thinking mind; if he heard me drop a word that he did not understand, I have known him think it over for hours, and then come to me and ask for an explanation of the word. Sometimes it was difficult for me to explain so that he could understand, without which he would not be satisfied, except I could divert his mind from the subject. For instance: in conversation at tea table, in reply to something which had been said, I said, "Yes at the conflagration of all things." After some time, he said, "Father, what does conflagration mean?" I said "When all things shall be burnt up." He left the table, and after reflecting upon it for some time, he came to me and said, "Father, how can the stone flags be burnt up?" I said, "I cannot tell how they will be burnt." Then, he said, "You should not say so." I thought, it will not do for him to understand that I have been telling him a falsehood. I said, "I cannot explain how the stones will be burnt, but it is said in the word of God 'The elements shall melt with fervent heat, the earth also and the works that are therein shall be burnt up'." He seemed not satisfied by a long way, and wanted to know when this would take place. I found in this case, as well as in others, I must divert his mind from the subject. He was a fine boy; take him every way, I never saw his equal. Our hopes in him were very great. His sufferings were great in the last few weeks of his life. This was a trying time for us, my wife felt it keenly, being with him night and day. And all efforts to save his life were abortive. He died in the month of October 1827, aged 4 years and 8 months. This was a sore trial to us. Though his afflictions had been severe, his death seemed sudden to us, for up to the time he had the measles he had enjoyed very good health, and our hopes were very great in him. But God who is too wise to err, and too good to be unkind, took him to himself. And may He help us so to live, that we may live with Him for ever, then we shall soon meet again to part no more.

This year, we had a revival of religion, and many added to our Society, and our business was also prospering. The Lord hath dealt bountifully with us both in things temporal and spiritual. I desire to adore him with all my soul, yea O my God, may I ever acknowledge Thee in all things for Christ's sake. Amen.

The Longholme Society, having engaged to take to Bacup Quarter-day three pounds per quarter, were in arrears thirty pounds. Only a few years before the new chapel was built and from that time (say about five or six years) to the year 1827, the Society had so improved that they had not only paid off their arrears, but were then sending to the Bacup Quarter-day ten pounds or more per quarter. They raised for the missionary cause in the same year by subscriptions £49. 14. 2, public collections £43. 0. 6, total £92. 14. 8 and in 1828, they raised for the missionary cause by subscriptions £53. 14. 0, public collections £52. 18. 9. total £102. 12. 9. William Dawson of Barnbow was then in his prime, and his equal for giving effect on a missionary platform I never heard. He was a great, good man.

YORKSHIRE TOUR

In September 1828 my wife and I had a most delightful tour in Yorkshire. We had a good horse and gig with us. [Here is a] copy of a letter to my brothers:

Hull, September 25th 1828.

Dear brothers,
On Saturday night we reached Bramley, and found Mr. and Mrs. Fish very well, with whom we remained Sunday over and spent the day very agreeably and profitable and had the pleasure of again hearing our late minister Mr. Fish preach. On Monday morning we proceeded through Leeds and called upon Mr. William Dawson, with whom we had the pleasure to dine. He took us through his farm, and we felt much interested to see the place where that great man lived. I delivered my mission to invite him to come to our missionary meeting. He did not say anything against coming, so I had nothing to say but get his time.

We arrived at Tadcaster the same night. The waiter appeared as if he was in a bad temper, and things were not so very pleasant. Tuesday morning we got to York about 8 o'clock, and were highly pleased in the Cathedral, while hearing "Creation" by Haydn and some of Handel's works, performed by about six hundred altogether of singers and players of musical instruments. We also heard the notable singer Madame Catalani.[5] (N.B. this was the last oratorio held in York Minster before it was burnt down). We went through the Minster and to the top of the castle. To the top of the Cathedral there are 107 steps, and to the top of the castle 161 steps, in all 268 steps. It is a fine building, the architecture good both internal and external.

We left York about five o'clock, went to Market Weighton, where we met with very comfortable entertainment. On Wednesday morning we went to Beverley, and were wonderfully surprised to find such a pretty town there with a Minster similar to that of York, but on a much smaller scale. We mounted up to the top of it, two hundred and two steps. This town, while we were in it, was the quietest I ever saw before. We saw very few persons in the streets, I think not one person in one hundred yards the town through, nor any carriage or cart or horse, except our own, and one cart which had no horse in it. At night we arrived at Hull, and got to a very good Inn, and had great attention paid to us. Their charges are low. We are very much interested with the town, ships, and the improvement they are now making in their docks. For the short time we have been here, we have enjoyed ourselves very much indeed. We intend to be at Harrogate on Monday. Please write to us on Saturday but don't seal up the letter till Manchester letter comes, and let me have the news from there, and let us know particulars how our children are, and if they are all well, as we are at present.

From your affectionate brother,
David Whitehead
To Thomas Whitehead and Brothers.

After spending about a week at Harrogate, we came home and found all our children and family well. What cause of thankfulness!

Let my soul praise and acknowledge God whose goodness and mercy has ever been with me and my family. There is no place like home, praise the Lord for home, and may He guide us and our children by his almighty hand to our eternal home with Jesus Christ our Redeemer and there sing "Worthy is the Lamb that was slain to receive power and riches and wisdom, and strength and honour, and glory and blessing. Blessing and honour and glory and power to be unto Him that sitteth upon throne for ever and ever." Amen.

Trade has not been quite so good this year, but God has made our business to prosper. In the beginning of the year 1829, Peter's wife's health began to fail, and on the 21st October she left brother Peter a widower with two children. A. Watmough, who was then stationed in Bacup Circuit preached a sermon on the occasion, after which he delivered the following brief memoir of her, viz:

The late Mrs. Peter Whitehead was the third daughter of the late Thos. Kay of Flaxmoss, near Haslingden. Mr. Kay was a member of the Methodist Society for a considerable number of years, and filled the office of Class Leader in the village where he resided and was also Steward of the Haslingden circuit. Mr. Kay was a truly good man, a Christian indeed, and he departed this life in the year 1821 in the full assurance of entering into that peace and rest which God has prepared above for those who love his name. Mr. Kay, being a man of God and wishful to promote the happiness of his children, was careful to instruct them in the ways of the Almighty and had the pleasure, even before his decease, of knowing that his labours were not in vain in the Lord.

The conduct of Alice, the subject of this memoir, was regular and steady during the earlier years of her life, and there is no doubt that she was also at that time the subject of gracious impressions and of desires and inclinations towards that which is good. But being somewhat reserved in her conversation, she seldom said much on the subject of her gracious impressions or the feelings and experience of her own mind. She became, however, a member of Society when about sixteen years of age, and regularly met in Class till the day of her death. At the time she entered into Society she was at a respectable boarding school near Frodsham, in Cheshire, where her parents had sent her more fully to qualify and prepare to fill her future station in life. When at this school the solicitude of her father to secure the everlasting welfare of his daughter was not suspended in its operations. In his letters to her he endeavoured to impress her mind with a sense of the superior importance of spiritual things. One of which now lies before me in which are contained the following words:

"I hope," says the father, "You will endeavour to pay all possible attention to your learning and be earnest in prayer that the Lord may bless your soul and make you happy in the enjoyment of religion." In another letter, which was written about half a year afterwards, I find the following words: "We are glad to hear you are in health, and hope you are improving in your learning, still considering that this is for your own benefit through life, and with all your learning be learning and walking in the way that leads to heaven." Her father then adds "Be earnest in secret prayer. Never omit that duty. For, if your friends do not see you, the Lord does and He will help you if you ask Him. Endeavour to get all the good you can by hearing the Gospel preached, by reading the Scriptures, by attending your Class Meeting and by a due regard to watchfulness and to family prayer."

Such was the written advice which Mrs. W. received while young and at school. And coming from a father to a well disposed child, and being followed, as they were, by fervent prayer to the Almighty, it was impossible they should not be productive of good. They must have had a salutary and happy effect and have tended to lead her still nearer to God.

She returned from school at the following vacation being then in her seventeenth year, and must have been grateful to the feelings of her parents that she returned from this seminary with testimonials of most excellent conduct furnished by the ladies who conducted that school. When she came home she continued to meet in Class and to attend the more public ordinances and means of grace. Her deportment was serious and steady and sincerity appeared to mark all her steps, yet she did not attain to the liberty of the children of God, or rise to that peace and happiness which others enjoyed. This was often a source of great uneasiness to her mind, and continued almost till her death to be an occasion of painful and perplexing temptation and deep distress. A want of clearer light on the plan of salvation was doubtless the principal cause of all this, for she appears to have been seeking salvation more by works of the law than by faith and she often perplexed and troubled herself by needlessly supposing that because her repentance had not been so deep as the repentance of many of whom she heard speak, she could not be justified, yet must wait for that blessing till her sorrow for sin was increased and her spirit more broken and humbled before God. Thus she lingered by the pool and declined to step in, and, though evidently longing for the blessing, refused to be whole.

In the month of November 1824 she entered the marriage state and came to reside at Rawtenstall where she continued till death. Her conduct was uniform and steady and such as rendered her agreeable to her increasing circle of friends, and in many things a pattern to those among whom she lived. She loved her husband, was fondly attentive to her children and eminently a keeper at home. She was humble, modest and sincere and delighted in the cause and people of God. The ministers of God she greatly respected and from a conviction of the great injury which it does to the cause of religion in general and to the souls of those who indulge in it, she would not join in any conversation which tended in the least to lessen the character or depreciate the talents (however weak) of those who preached the glad tidings of peace to the souls of men. And happy will they be who may learn from this account to imitate our departed sister in this respect.

But it not infrequently happens that our brightest prospects are soon overcast with clouds of darkness and disappointment and the star of our hope goes down from our vision before it has well begun to shine, and this was the case with respects to that lamented individual of whom I am giving this contracted account. She had been comfortably settled in life in her twenty-first year, was becoming a mother of children, and enjoyed a considerable portion of health and strength, seldom complaining of any bodily indisposition till about the beginning of January 1829. About that period, however, she experienced some declension in her appetite, yet did not consider herself particularly unwell till about the beginning of the month of April, when she was under the necessity of taking [to] her bed, and was confined for several weeks.

Towards the conclusion of the month of May, however, she recovered a little and acquired a portion of her wonted strength so as to take several rides in the country, which did not, however, afford her any relief. During this affliction her mind was deeply exercised on the all important subject of religion and she was often in considerable distress respecting her own state of mind, for she did not as yet, though she had been in Society, for several years, experience a sense of her personal acceptance with God. She had sometimes on former occasions when musing on her spiritual state, and sensible she had not been sufficiently in earnest about spiritual things, indulged an inward desire to suffer affliction, with the hope of being roused thereby with stronger and greater degrees of exertion for spiritual good. And her merciful Father pitied her condition and granted the desire of her soul in that respect. She was now suffering under affliction and her bodily affliction was becoming a means of spiritual good. [She] was stirred up to seek the Lord and cried mightily to him for help, yet she could not subdue her doubts and fears & rise superior to unbelief. She looked at the experience of others, whose convictions of sin and sorrow had been greater than her own and indulged the mistaken idea that pardon and peace were not to be obtained by her till she had bled under sorrows as bitter as theirs and drunken a similar portion of anguish and distress. In consequence of this, instead of looking for pardon and acceptance through faith in a crucified Redeemer, she was daily looking and looking for more conviction and distress and grieving because she thought she did not grieve enough.

Thus she continued till about June of the present year, when her insidious affliction, after a temporary abatement of its severity, had fully resumed its formidable appearance again, and was threatening to lay its victim in the dust. Her husband and her were conversing on the state of her mind, when he endeavoured to call to her recollection the necessity of faith in the Lord Jesus and the unreasonableness of doubt and unbelief. He spoke of the sufferings of Christ to save her and of the promises of pardon through faith in His blood, and he requested her to consider what dishonour was done to God by doubting the promises He had thus made to man. At the close of this conversation she said she would try to consider these things afresh and endeavour to cast her whole soul upon the merits of Christ, which accordingly she did. Nor was this struggle for life in vain in the Lord. She obtained a degree of comfort by simply relying on Christ and believed her soul accepted of God.

Nevertheless, she lost this confidence again in two or three days and fell into doubt and distressing again. But this advantage which the enemy of her soul got over her was happily of but transient duration. In the space of about a week, by a renewed act of faith in the Lord Jesus, she experienced the return of that peace which invariably results from the soul's reliance upon the atoning blood of the Son of God. This peace, however, in the case of Mrs. W. was not attended with those lively and vivid transports of joy which many experience when just brought to God. Neither did the peace itself always flow like a river swelling and filling its banks; it was a calmly flowing stream carrying away the fear and dread of death from her soul, but admitting at the same time of an abounding increase, and disposing her to cry daily for brighter displays of the power and grace of the Son of God. So that her state of mind at that time, her mingled feelings of confidence and desire, her genuine, though weak, faith, mixed with the expiring remains of unbelief, may well be expressed in the following lines of our poet who seems to have well understood cases of this kind:

> "I hold Thee with a trembling hand,
> But will not let Thee go.
> Till steadfastly by faith I stand
> And all Thy goodness know."

And again,

"Come then my God, mark out Thine heir,
Of heaven a larger earnest give;
With clearer light Thy witness bear,
More sensibly within me live.
Let all my powers Thine entrance feel,
And deeper stamp Thyself the seal."

It is natural to suppose that as her affliction increased upon her and the clouds of mortality thickened on every side that her mind would sometimes be exercised with the thought of leaving her friends, but particularly her husband and her babes in the world. And perhaps it is not easy for the living to conceive what the dying must experience when compelled to turn their attention to those things. Many a tender mother would feel the severity of the stroke if compelled to leave their children for a month. But to be separated by death to be removed from their embrace and from the sight of their countenance, to see them no more in the land of the living, would be a stroke that would prove intolerable to be borne if grace for so trying an occasion were not given from God. Mrs. Whitehead, however, as the time of her dissolution drew nigh, was completely delivered from distress and anxiety about everything pertaining to this present world and could cheerfully resign her children and her husband into the hands of a merciful and promise-keeping God. This enabled her to devote her thoughts more exclusively to the concerns of that eternity towards which she appeared now to be rapidly hastening, when she was to close her eyes for ever on all the objects below. And it was pleasing to her friends that, though her joy, even to the last, was not rapturous & transporting, yet her trust and confidence in the Lord seemed daily to acquire strength as the time of her departure drew near, and that she finished her course in peace and with a firm and unshaken reliance upon the Saviour's atoning blood.

Thus lived, and thus died, in the twenty-sixth year of her age, the late Mrs. Whitehead of whom it may justly be said she came up like a flower and was cut down, she fled also as a shadow and continued not. May her untimely decease be sanctified to our good, and maybe all meet her at last in the Kingdom above.

In 1830 A. Watmough appointed brother Thomas a Class Leader.

CANADIAN MERCHANTS

In the year 1830, we became merchants. We established a house at Montreal in Canada, in connection with Thomas Kay and David Lacy. Thomas Kay was brother to brother Peter's late wife, a young man who we had been training up in our business. He had a desire to go abroad. He was a young man in whom I felt a great interest so we went into partnership with him and David Lacy as merchants and they both went out to Montreal, Canada, and established a house in the dry goods business. After David Lacy had been out about one year, he drew out of the business and returned home. Thomas Kay still remaining in the business, the firm was then carried on in the name of Kay, Whitehead and Co., Montreal, and Whitehead, Kay and Co., Rawtenstall.

In the Spring of each year I spent a good deal of time in buying goods suitable for that market. We had our hands quite full in business but found it a privilege to give a regular and proper time to religion and the cause of God.

The time began to draw near when our Circuit would have according to the engagement made with the Conference, to take a married second preacher. At our Quarter-day the numbers were looked up, and an urgent request made for every Society to bring money to the Quarter-day, according to their numbers in Society. We said we had at Longholme Chapel, Rawtenstall, a large number of schoolchildren in Society, perhaps one hundred or more, who paid nothing at all to the Society. They said that was a loss to the circuit, because they would bring an additional charge upon it, the circuit. I was a strong advocate for schoolchildren to be brought into the church. Nothing tends more to the prosperity of a church than to get the young into the church. Bacup Circuit had never been a pauper to the funds of the Wesleyan Connection or Conference, nor ever did we intend it to be. After a good deal of conversation at Quarter-day and elsewhere, we as a Circuit came to the conclusion that we would raise a fund which should be laid upon the chapels in the Circuit; the fund so raised to be divided after the rate of so much per pound to each chapel according to the debt on each chapel. To be laid on at three percent per annum, and the Trustees of each chapel to give a promissory note to the Bacup Circuit, Stewards in office, and the Trustees to pay the interest to the Stewards of the Circuit every year and if the Circuit Stewards should need the interest or any part of the interest for the wants of the circuit, the Stewards should take what was needed and what the Stewards did not need to be returned back to each chapel its share towards lessening the debts of such chapels. A subscription was entered into as follows:

J. R. Kay of Longholme	£100
Thomas Whitehead of Rawtenstall	£100
David Whitehead of Hall Hill	£100
Peter Whitehead of Rawtenstall	£100
Thomas Kay of Longholme	£105
John Earnshaw of Bacup	£100
Edmund Dawson of Bacup	£100
and other smaller sums	£391. 17. 10.

This fund amounted to the sum of £1,096. 17. 10. So then we could keep into Society our schoolchildren, and train them up for Heaven. I was a Trustee for Bacup Chapel, but not for any other, but Abm. Watmough, our Minister, got new deeds made for Newchurch Chapel, Rakefoot Chapel, and Longholme Chapel, Rawtenstall, in which my brothers, T & P and I were all made Trustees in each Chapel.

Brother Peter was married again March 14th, 1832 to Elizabeth Kay a daughter of John Kay of Goodshawfold, Cotton Manufacturer. He was a Wesleyan Methodist and Class Leader, and Society Steward for Rakefoot who felt a great interest in that Society and the Circuit at large. He was Trustee for several chapels, and a pious, good man. This year, 1832, brother Peter was appointed a Class Leader, so our Society continued to increase, praise the Lord.

The Trustees of Longholme Chapel, Rawtenstall, built a new house at Rawtenstall for the second preacher, towards which brothers Thomas, Peter and I gave ninety pounds. The Bacup Circuit was then fully prepared for a second married preacher, and in this year, 1832, L. Barlow and W. Brailsford were stationed in the Bacup Circuit, two good preachers. They were a good pair, worked well together, though not both the same in their political views. I have had many conversations with them both together which I enjoyed very much indeed. We had much good feeling and union in the Circuit. W. Brailsford laboured hard to establish an Auxiliary Bible Society in the neighbourhood, in which he succeeded, viz: comprising Rawtenstall, Newchurch and Bacup. All the three places together were found not to work well, so Mr. Brooke, one of the agents of the parent Society, came to Rawtenstall, and divided the Society, and established one at Rawtenstall and another at Bacup. He called a public meeting at Rawtenstall. I was requested to be the President of the Rawtenstall Auxiliary Bible Society, which I cheerfully accepted. We also established a Ladies' Association which worked well with the Auxiliary Society.

PARLIAMENTARY ELECTIONS

I received from Mr. A. Watmough the following letter.

Leicester, December 21st, 1832.

Mr. D. Whitehead,

My Dear Brother,

Old acquaintance, and friendship, and recollections of past interviews and pleasures, which I have often had with you both in the house of God, and at Hall Hill, demands the tribute of a letter. Which, indeed, I am afraid, will but very ill discharge the obligation I feel under to you, because, to say the truth, I generally feel so ill able to write letters that are worthy of the perusal of my friends, that I utterly despair even to cancel my obligation in that sort of way. However, as I have promised to write to you, and find it will afford to myself no ordinary pleasure, by calling to my remembrance persons and places and things with which I had formerly had to do, I sit down to prepare you a short letter, which I hope, by the kindness of the Almighty, will find you in health.

But what shall be the subject of my epistle? I can tell you sincerely and truly, that I am tolerably well, that Mrs. W. is the same, that we have good congregations, that we have had some conversions to God, some back sliders reclaimed, some increase in the prayer meetings, and in some of our class meetings, and the like. And that I feel a sacred pleasure in striving, to the best of my ability, to promote a still further increase in all these good things.

I can state all this to you sincerely enough, but then I stated these things in substance in my late letter to your brother, so that there is nothing at all new, and therefore nothing at all interesting in any of these things I think, therefore, I had best leave these things unnoticed in this letter, and turn my attention to one or two of the many and interesting topics in the which I am fully persuaded you find permanent delight. I am fully persuaded that my letter will be welcome if I only remind you of a great and solemn event which is daily drawing near, that is the termination of trade and commerce and the like: and that a new state of things is about to commence in which they will neither marry nor be given in marriage, nor sell nor get any worldly gain. Indeed they will have no motive to incline them, nor any interest whatsoever to induce them, to desire in the least, or for one single moment to seek after, either the gold or silver and other treasures of this present world, for they will be of no service whatsoever in that new state of things to which I refer. When you and I and all who are near and dear to each of us shall come into that new state of things, there is one thing and only one which will be of any service to us, and that is a certain state or qualification of mind and heart, such a qualification, I mean, as will enable us to worship and serve and love and adore God in spirit and in truth. For, as this quality or state of mind is the only state for which there will be any imployment in that new order of things which is every day drawing nearer and nearer, at least for such as will be happy there, so of course this is the only thing, amidst all the variety of objects which now occupy our thoughts and attention, which will be of any use at all in that future state to which I refer. This, then, will be the only thing worthy of attention. And this state of mind will not be acquirable in that new order of things where it will be so infinitely necessary, but must be acquired before we enter upon it if we ever do obtain it, so, it will be wise to give all diligence now, while it may be sought after with success, that we may attain unto it, you see how my thoughts run on. My pen follows very limpingly, but you have got the end of the clue; and you may now follow it to any extent you think fit. Since the time I began to write you this letter, two or three weeks have run off into eternity, and have given breath to many bubbles of life, which have appeared for a moment on its move, then burst and vanished away.

The last week but this which is now drawing to a close, we have been bustling in the Borough with a contested election. Leicester sends two members to Parliament, and we had three candidates, two Whigs and one Tory. The Tory was brought forward by the Corporation, headed by the Mayor, but although they have never lost a contested election before, for the last 60 years, and have used on the present occasion, all the influence they have or could possibly muster up, the two Whigs are returned. The election occasioned for the time a good deal of excitement, but we had no tumult, no uproar no confusion, all was done orderly and in peace. They were both chaired on Friday (a week since today) and the day after (Saturday), the two members for the Southern Division of the County were both quietly returned. There was no opposition and one of them was chaired on the afternoon of that day. The other declined the offer of being chaired being a Tory in principle, he feared to ride through the populace of Leicester in their present state of triumphant excitement, though I hope they are too moderate and peaceable to have done him any harm. Will the new Parliament be able to do us any good so long as our national vices abound? I for one am afraid they will not. *Their intentions*, I doubt not, will be directed to this end, but I hear a voice saying "Your iniquities have separated between you and your God, and your sins have held good things from you." And I believe that voice to be true and faithful.

I seem to have nothing to add to the above, save my kind and brother respects to – whom? Why, to *all* of you to be sure, both at Hall Hill and at Rawtenstall, not forgetting the little daughters and sons at both of the places. Write soon and tell me how you all are. I had rather *bring* this letter than *send* it, but O! we cannot *now* have everything we wish. Tell Mr. and Mrs. P that I think of writing to them soon, only I should like first to be indulged with a letter from you – we have some souls brought to God, but not so many as I should like to see. I hope it is still well with you. The Lord be with you. Amen. Mrs Watmough joins cordially in all respects to all. I wish I had time to write a neater letter than this scribble will be found, but I hope you will excuse it. You know what I am.

    Your ever dutiful friend and brother in Christ,
        A. Watmough

Through the multiplicity of business, I neglected answering the above letter until January 19th /33.

        Hall Hill, January 19th 1833.

Mr. Watmough.
My dear Brother

It is with no small degree of pleasure I take up my pen to acknowledge the reception of your much esteemed favour of the 21st December, 1832, which duly came to hand. The perusal of it, I can assure you, brought a-many pleasing things to my recollection I hope never to be forgotten. The last Quarter-day meeting with you at Newchurch is yet fresh in my memory. I felt at that Quarter-day as I never felt on any former of a similar kind. I feel myself quite inadequate to make a suitable reply to your interesting letter. What with the agitation of business, the things of this world, calculations, care &c. I find it takes some time to procure a calm mind. For when I seem to have some leisure time, my mind is something like the great deep after a storm or gale of wind. For I have more than once sat down to write to you, and by the time I got anything like fit to write, another interruption broke out, and I have had to rise again without accomplishing anything. So that in writing this letter, I have more than ordinary pleasure, for every attempt has brought to my mind pleasing circumstances. Therefore, I shall proceed, having no doubt but you will pardon me for all errors and bad arrangement.

    Trade and commerce I still pursue with delight, although it is not all straightforward, and I am quite convinced I am in the way providence designed for me. But you say, and say truly too, the termination of these things are daily and hourly drawing near. O! what a great blessing that God has so ordered it that it is our privilege to enjoy these things while passing through time, and still ready to give them up, when God in His wisdom shall cause a separation. I feel thankful that I am able to say I feel no intanglement here below, but happy in the knowledge of the love and goodness of God, and a blessed hope of enjoying my Saviour for ever in another world. I have read your epistle over more than once, and am very much obliged to you for it, and particularly upon the subject I have just hinted at, viz.: the termination of the things of this world which is absolutely the case with John Whitehead, brother Thomas' eldest son, who died of water in the brain at Doncaster the 26th ult., and on the 29th was brought to Rawtenstall and interred in their family vault. He was a fine boy, fourteen years old, and promised fair for this world, but all these promises are blasted. The affliction was great to his parents, which, I am happy to say, they passed through with Christian fortitude. His mother is better than when you left us. My family and self, brothers and sisters, are all well, with the exception of some slight colds. They all desire me to send their kind regards to you and Mrs. Watmough.

The last Quarter-day was a very interesting one, the Circuit is in spiritual health, but not any increase that I am aware of. I would just say the contributions towards the new house and furnishing the same which were brought to Quarter-day, in addition to what were promised when you were with us, were upwards of one hundred pounds. I am quite clear of this, that God gives to us to give, and blesses us when we give; and has a particular care over those that do give. My prayers that God may still bless us, and make us a blessing – and not us only, but all the churches. And the same divine goodness be given to yourself.

I feel as if I could write to you all day, but I must come to a conclusion for the present. But, I must not forget to inform you that my wife got another fine boy about 9 or 10 weeks ago, and she and the child have been doing very well till within about a week or ten days. I think they have got a slight cold, but hope they will be quite well in a few days. She joins me in love to you and Mrs. Watmough, and I beg you will favour me at some future time with another long epistle. I would just say, we like our preachers well. Mr. Brailsford removed to the new house last Tuesday, and Mrs. B was confined on the Wednesday night. She has got a fine boy and they are doing very well at present.

Excuse all the faults and brevity.
I remain your affectionate friend and brother in Christ,
David Whitehead.

Our business has been increasing both at home and abroad. Mr. Thomas Kay, our partner at Montreal, had been corresponding with Miss Lacy of Stoodley, near Todmorden, whom he was anxious to make his wife. He came over from Montreal to England, and in the Spring of 1833 was married to Miss Lacy, on the 5th March and took her back with him to Montreal. While he was over, I was very busy indeed, going with him buying goods to send out with him, and sometimes going with him to see his intended. At the same time my brothers and I were in contemplation and in treaty with Mr. Law about a mill, some cottage houses, and an estate of land, all at Rawtenstall which we succeeded in buying.

Mr. and Mrs. Kay left Liverpool for Montreal, Canada, in the beginning of April 1833, so my time has been fully occupied for the last three or four months. I wrote to Mr. Kay by the following packet to Montreal, giving him a little advice, as it was my custom to do a little that way as well as on business, viz:

Liverpool. April 13th, 1833.
Mr. Thomas Kay,
Montreal.
My dear sir,

I have for some years felt myself deeply interested for your welfare, I think as much so as if you had been my own child. The reason or cause why I should is unknown to me, perhaps I may know in another world.

From the same feeling, I take up my pen to give you a word of advice, which if you take, I feel confident will be of service to you, both for this world and another. As you have now taken to yourself a partner in life which I have no doubt will be made a blessing to your soul, strive to do each other good by living near to God, and be not too anxious for this world. If you be, you will not get as much of it, because you will not know how to use it right. Recollect we are not made for this world, but for another and a better.

I do not mean you are not to be diligent in your business but, when you have done your best according to your judgement, and have been careful to collect all the knowledge you can as regards the things you are engaged in, then leave the event to God.

You have prayed for a wife, God has heard and answered your prayers and why should you be faithless as regards other things? In your domestic affairs be careful, waste nothing, save all you can. Live not in high life, do away naughty pride, but live comfortable. Nothing will enable you to manage your domestic affairs so well as religion. If you always live with a knowledge of the witness of the Spirit you will be able to know what is right. Cultivate a desire to help the cause of God, both by your influence and money.

Excuse my Freedom, but forget it not. You have this from the sincerity of my heart.

David Whitehead.

HOLLY MOUNT

After this, brother Peter and I set our heads and hands to work in planning the grounds and the buildings of Holly Mount, which we built upon the estate of land bought from Mr. Law. It is difficult to describe the land as it was before we bought it, but, standing at the south door of Holly Mount observatory, the ground was just that height, and nearly the same in height for about 20 yards square, declining a little more towards the west than the south for the space of the fore-mentioned 20 yards. And then the decline was more rapid southwards all the way to the road, except a few yards towards the bottom, but not so quick a decline westwards. On the north-east of the observatory the decline was very rapid down to the river, in which there was a quantity of large, massive stones, from which I am inclined to think Rawtenstall took its name. For I think it was called by the Saxons, or in German language "Routounds clough", perhaps through the noise the water made in going through these stones; and when they came on their hunting excursions in the Forest of Rossendale they made Booths or Stalls, from which they might call this place "Rawtenstall."

Brother Peter and I fixed upon this spot, just before the south door of Holly Mount Observatory, the highest part of the ground, and drove a pile of wood down into the ground, from which we took all our levels for excavation, removing part of the hill, and forming the ground and buildings of Holly Mount. Brother Peter and I were the architects. I drew all the plans and designs, and brother Peter assisted in designing and carrying them out. He was the best for mental calculation I ever met with. I took my head and my pen, and he his head, and we worked together and if I made a mistake in calculation, he generally could tell. One time we took dimensions of a very awkward quantity of earth to be removed; which we were going to let to be removed. I calculated the whole up by decimals and told him the number of yards which I made it. He said he made it half a yard more. I examined my figures over, and found to my astonishment he was right. How he had ascertained the right number of yards even to a few decimal fractions, by mental calculation, I could not tell.

In forming and preparing the ground for Holly Mount buildings were moved 19,664 cube yards of earth. Before we removed this earth, we took the depths and calculated the amount to be removed. The men to whom we let the work took the depths as they removed the earth, and found it to be the same number of yards we had told them. Part of the houses and all the outbuildings were built from stone out of our own quarry on the same estate. The stones of the front and each end of the three houses came from Dean Clough near Padiham.

On the 3rd of April 1834 we laid the first stone of the base course, south corner, of the three houses, and christened the place on which they stand "Holly Mount". Its name before this was called Copse.

In the month of August 1834 my sister Alice was married to the Rev. Battinson Kay. A number of females (eight or ten Wesleyan Methodists, who met in class together) of whom she was the leader, after which my wife was appointed the leader of this class of females.

WESLEYAN METHODIST DISPUTE

About this time there was much dissatisfaction in the Wesleyan Connection through their establishing the Theological Institution. We in Bacup Circuit got up a petition to send to the conference against the Theological Institution. But W. Tranter, being then Superintendent of Bacup Circuit, would not pass our petition as chairman of the circuit. Mr. Thomas Kay of Longholme and his son J. R. Kay were strong opponents to the Theological Institution, and so were all the Bacup Circuit. Some were for withholding the money at Quarter-day if Mr. Tranter would not pass the petition. I said, "No, we will not do that. But if Mr. Tranter will not pass the petition, let us bring a charge against him at the District Meeting, then the District meeting will have to see the petition or would have to know the reason why Mr. Tranter would not pass it. And if the District will not order him to pass it, then bring a charge against him at the Conference for objecting to pass our petition. By this means, our petition will have more notice taken of if it went quietly to Conference."

Brother Peter was then the Circuit Steward. He took the petition to the District meeting and a charge was brought against Mr. Tranter. The petition was well read amongst the preachers, for many were anxious to know what kind of a petition it was, seeing there was such a stir about it. After brother Peter had stopped at District meeting a day or two, they told him that the Meeting would have nothing to do with it, and the Circuit and Mr. Tranter might act as they thought proper. But after Mr. Tranter came back, he called a Meeting, and passed the petition, and the petition went to Conference. If all the Circuits had been like Bacup Circuit, there would have been no splits in the Methodist Society, but Methodism conserved. For I consider Bacup Circuit a conserver and their money and advice they bestow wherever they think it will do good, but never goes to the funds of the Connection for money. They know it is more blessed to give than receive.

I object to the Theological Institution because it is too much upon the centralising system, concentrated powers, virtually over the Conference. Then, again, it does not require, generally, a learned, man to preach the gospel. It does require a pious, good, common-sense man. John Wesley was right in sending the boys to school; but I doubt whether it is right to send a man to school whom God has called to preach the gospel. [D.W. then shifts to a sermon he remembers].

God took Moses when a little boy and sent him to Pharaoh's daughter, who gave him an Egyptian education of first rate. And it came to pass, when Moses was grown up, that God in his providential way sent him to Jethro to take care of his flock and learn farming a bit. Then God called him to be a leader and teacher of his people, and when God wanted at another time a learned man He called Paul.

I am as much for the education of the right sort as any man. Educate the young children and up to men, while God call them (such as He will) to preach His gospel, and don't mar them afterwards by sending them to school. They may learn Methodism but I doubt whether preaching so as to be more productive of the salvation of souls. And if the Theological Institution [is] ever be of any service to the Wesleyan Methodist it must be differently constituted. A school should have no power over the Church of God, no more than the State. They are of this world, and Christ is the Head of the Church, and the Church can acknowledge neither school nor State as their head, neither to rule nor to legislate.

We in the Bacup Circuit told our mind freely to the Conference, and kept firmly together and to what we believed to be the best for Methodism had no splits or division. Not that I think divisions are always bad, for it perhaps might not be so well for religion in England if we had only one Methodist Conference, but we have Wesleyan Methodist, New Connection Methodist, Primitive Methodist and Wesleyan Association Methodist, each holding a Conference. If the Wesleyan Methodists had had no divisions, they might be so foolish as to build a Babel, and God in mercy may yet confound a Society in their language when they are going wrong so that they cannot understand one another, and so scatter them abroad upon the face of all the earth. God is too wise to err and too good to be unkind. His goodness and mercy are still with us.

LOWER MILL, 1833

We have been employing for some time more than fifty masons, labourers and quarry men. There has been many dangers, but no one killed thanks be to God. After we had built the three houses, Holly Mount, we three brothers cast lots for them, and each took the house which fell to him by lot, and we were all well satisfied each with his own lot. I removed my family from Hall Hill to Holly Mount in the month of October 1835.

We continued to employ the masons, labourers, &c and went on with our contemplated plan, to prepare the ground for building our Rawtenstall Lower Mill. The ground for this mill and Holly Mount cost us more to prepare it for building than we gave for the ground itself. We covered the river for about 212 yards with an arch 22 feet wide; and another arch of the same size from the head of the water wheel about 50 yards long and also another arch from the tail of the water wheel about 9 feet wide and 109 yards long. We pulled down the old Mill, a size house, and seven or eight cottage houses, bought from Mr. Law and Thomas Howorth. On the same ground, and across the river, we built our Rawtenstall Lower Mill, consisting of buildings for spinning, sizing or dressing twist, power loom weaving, warehouses, &c ample for upwards of eight hundred power looms, and gas works to supply these works and our Rawtenstall Higher Mill, and other buildings and shops &c.

At the end of the weaving shed, we built a school, and a tower for a clock for the works, with five faces, viz: one face in the weaving shed, and a face on each side of the tower, some one of which or more can be seen from the works and inside of the mill, from Holly Mount, from within the school, and by the public. While building these buildings and a large number of cottage houses, brother Peter and I being our own architects, we had to be very diligent, having all the designs and plans to get out, and superintend the work as it went on. And we had our business as Manufacturers and Merchants to attend to beside. But we did not think that were all for which we came into the world, to be builders, manufacturers and merchants. No, we thought there were a great deal more for us to do, both in religion, politics, and other useful institutions.

We saw the working class were spending their money, for which they had laboured hard, in intoxicating drink, and starving their poor children. We came to the conclusion, when we began to build Holly Mount, which we still adhere to, that we would not allow any footings amongst our masons or labourers, nor any intoxicating drink to be brought upon the ground to be drunk in company one with another. Nor would we give any intoxicating drink at floor layings or rearings. But on all such occasions we would give the allowance in money to each man, or a dinner to them altogether. In that case, we allowed one pint of beer to each man.

The next or second dinner we gave in this way, the landlord with whom we contracted for their dinners said he must have three pence per man more for their dinners, for "Your masons do not drink after dinner, as other masons!" and that he could not afford them at the same price. We told him we were very glad, and that he must make a full charge, and let the men have a good dinner.

Brother Peter and I were constantly lecturing the men upon sobriety and economy, so that it became a rare thing for any of our masons to miss a day's work an account of drinking. Some who had been drunkards became sober men, other masons came and desired to be employed by us, alleging that our masons did not

Lower Mill and Holly Mount

drink like other masons who had footings and received their wages at public houses, and had drink for floor layings and rearings, and had very often a part of their wages to spend in drink; which they did not like.

One day, when in conversation with Mr. Ford (a gentleman in the neighbourhood) about these things, I remarked to him that it would be a good thing if we could get a bank for savings established in Rawtenstall. And he and brothers and I called a meeting, and formed a committee to carry out the object. We were successful in establishing a bank for savings in Rawtenstall viz: August 6th 1836. Though this bank was not established without much work and time being spent upon it, some of the more ignorant part of the workpeople said we should not be at all that trouble about it but we were going to have some benefit out of it. One day, when I was advising one of our workmen, who was getting a very good wage, to save some money and put it into the savings bank in order to be a help to him when more advanced in life, he said, "Nay, I am against savings banks." I said "Why?" "Well," he said, "You trade folks gets the money that poor folks puts in, to carry on your trade, and it is not for the benefit of working people, but for your benefit. You would not have been at all that trouble to get a savings bank if you were not to have the benefit yourselves." "Well", said I, "Upon the ground of that argument see how you are missing your way in spending your money wastefully, instead of putting it into the savings bank. For if tradesmen have to get money from the savings bank to carry on their trade then they become the employers of those who put their money into the savings bank, by employing their money and paying them interest for it. And if they cannot carry on trade without such money see what an injury you are doing to trade by not saving your money and putting it into the savings bank. For if there is no trade you can get no work; and if no work, no wages. But you think we should not be at all this trouble, if savings banks were not for our benefit. They are for our benefit, and for the benefit of all honest people who intend to pay their way. Just hear what shopkeepers say when we want anything for less than they offer them to us. Do they not tell us that they have a deal of money owing, and some never pay at all, and they cannot sell for less? And you know that it is common for workpeople to get into debt, some of them ten pound, some twenty pound, and some thirty pound or more. Some leave the country and never pay, and some die, and therefore their debts are lost. Shopkeepers have hundreds and thousands of pounds of these kind of debts owing and never will be paid. So, you see, honest men that pay their way have these debts to pay too. For shopkeepers continue to live. But how could they, if they did not charge more for what they have to sell?

"Now, we think, if we can get workpeople to save money when trade is good and full work, and put their savings into the bank, they will have something to take too, when trade is bad, or old age comes on; and thereby be able to pay their way and to go honourably through the world. And shopkeepers will be able to sell their goods cheaper, and live as well as they do. We who do pay our way will not have so much to pay for what we have to buy. Then I say is it not for our benefit to have banks for savings, to get workpeople to save money and put it into the bank too, because it will grow there (that is, it will accumulate interest), so that you will have more to take out than you put in?"

In this way, brother Peter and I availed ourselves of every opportunity amongst our workpeople, to instruct them. We also encouraged the Temperance Society, and got as many as we could of our neighbours to join it, and often attended their meetings, and gave them a little money to help them forward in that good cause.

In the year 1838, brother Peter told me he had been a teetotaller for about three years, and found his health be improved. I had been nearly a teetotaller for about ten years so that I did not drink a gallon of any kind of intoxicating drink in twelve months. I then made up my mind to be a complete teetotaller, and found it to be a very good thing for me; for I had often to say to my friends when they invited me to take a glass "Thank you, I would rather not". Sometimes, through much entreaty, and sooner than give offence, I took a glass, for some would have said "Are you a teetotaller?" and when I said "No", some would have gone so far as to say, "Why, have you something against me that you won't take a glass with me?" So, I found in such cases, when I could say, "I am a teetotaller," it at once set all at rest and beside, I could advocate temperance better amongst our workpeople, as it has always been my plan, when an opportunity might offer, to throw out something which might improve the working class. They are a fine class, and I have often thought, what a pity they do not understand economy better! That is a branch of education which school does not teach, but I feel it to be my duty to teach it wherever I can. As we continued to employ about fifty men for building, say masons and labourers, I often had an opportunity to speak to the men about these things.

The Wesleyan Society had increased so much in the neighbourhood that we had about as many members in Society as sittings in the Chapel. It was thought advisable to have a new Chapel. But it takes sometime to talk about these things before we can get all in one mind, and warmed up, so as to build properly when the time comes. Some thought it was too soon to build, and that we should take only a part of the scholars to the Chapel at a time, but for one I said that all the schoolchildren should go, and if there were not room enough for the adults, they must build a new Chapel, for the children could not build one; and it having been agreed upon by the Leaders and Teachers, soon after this Chapel was built, for the Sunday School children to attend divine worship morning and afternoon in this Chapel. I would not consent as one of the trustees for the children to be deprived of that privilege. The Society continued to prosper, and in the year 1839, my wife was appointed Leader, in addition to her Thursday Class, to a Sunday class of females, which she had raised out of the Sunday School. This year, a Wesleyan Chapel was built at Stacksteads, towards which my brothers and I gave thirty pounds, and ten pounds towards a Primitive Methodist Chapel at Crawshawbooth.

In the same year, 1839, brothers and I built our day school, viz: Holly Mount School, which cost us about one thousand pounds, consisting of two school rooms, one for males and another for females, and a committee room. We were anxious to give the best possible education to the working class, and particular to our workpeople. Therefore, we got from the Borough Road School, London, a male teacher and a female teacher.

We also felt anxious that the rising generation of workpeople should form habits of economy and of saving a part of their earnings when young. And with a view to induce our workpeople to do so, we established a Provident Trust, for the benefit of certain scholars attending Holly Mount School. All children who came to this school paid for their own education, say what was usual at such schools. But we signified to the above Trust that we would pay over to the agent of this Trust all monies for schooling by all scholars attending Holly Mount School as belonged to families some part of whom are in our employ yet reserving to ourselves the right, if we should hereafter see proper, to discontinue such payment; but should this ever be the case, still all monies previously placed to the credit of each scholar, to be faithfully paid over, to him or her, or their legal representatives.

The Trust were to put all such monies into the savings bank, and when, or as each child became twenty-one years old to have the monies at their credit with interest paid to them, or, if dead before, to their legal representatives. Any of these children were at liberty, if they chose, to put more than their school wages into this Provident Trust. There is a real pleasure in spending a little money and doing good this way.

MISER HOLT

What a difference between a mind of this kind and the mind of a poor miser! A miser who lived in our neighbourhood of Rossendale, died this year, 1840. Having been trained by his father Mr. Holt of Loveclough and mother to be a miser, report says that he surpasses his ancestors in that way, who were worth their tens of thousands of pounds, yet his mother said she could not tell what would become of James after her death fearing he (viz: Mr. Holt their only child) would not be able to keep himself. I have been told that when she died like she had some hundreds of pounds put by privately, which she had saved out of her egg money. She had a board with holes in, which she tried her eggs, and those eggs which would not go through the less holes were sold for more money, or kept for her own use. She survived her husband, so when she died, Mr. Holt her son had to attend to the funeral. It was usual in their family, at such times, to give a dinner at public house after the interment. He therefore went to most of the public houses in Haslingden to see who would give way most from their usual price, and give the dinner for the least money. Mr. Gray the clergyman told me that he came to him to know what he would charge for interring his mother. He told him, "the usual dues." But, Mr. Holt said he would not give it and that if he would not do it for less he would stick his mother in at Goodshaw Chapel. Mr. Gray told him if he did he would charge him the dues, and make him pay them too. Mr. Holt dressed as mean as any labouring man. He broke stones on the road, he got old cast-off clothes from any gentleman he could in the neighbourhood, he lived on very coarse food, and very likely his house would not cost him more than a few shillings per week. He had no wife, and his house keeper was of the same stamp as himself; and if Old Holt (that was the name he generally went by) had been from home, when he came back they reckoned every halfpenny he had spent. If he had spent too much, she would scold him. If he happened to go so far that he would not be back till night, she would make him some sad water porridge, and wrap them up in a cloth, which he took into his pocket for his dinner, and in some edge-side of the road or field, he would sit down and eat them for his dinner. A distant relation of his told me that he (Old Holt) coming through Accrington one night called upon him. He thought most likely he would want a bed; but had some company that night, he could not give him a bed, but took him to a public house and got him to bed. But the landlord asked him to pay for it, as he should not like to have anything to do with Old Holt about it. So he paid him for the bed, and Holt and him had each a glass of something to drink. When Holt paid for his glass, he had to get change for some silver. After he got home and had looked up his money, he found, or thought he was, two pence halfpenny short. He went back all the way next morning from Loveclough to Accrington, to inquire of his relation if the landlord gave him the right change, or how change he gave him as he was two pence halfpenny short. Holt would drink till he was drunk if somebody else would pay for the drink, but he did not like to pay for any himself.

Once at a town's meeting, after business of the meeting was over, the meeting thought they should have each a glass of spirits for the good of the house, which they would each have to pay for himself. It was agreed upon, and the glasses ordered in. Old Holt got up, said nothing, went out, but did not take his hat. The glasses came in, but Holt did not return. When they came to pay, they wanted the Landlord to take Old Holt's hat for his glass. "Nay", says the landlord, "I take my house from him. I will have nothing to do with Mr. Holt, you must pay me for what you ordered."

When the Church Chapel at Goodshaw was rebuilt, one of the churchwardens told me that he, along with another churchwarden, had had many trials to get a subscription from Old Holt but never could succeed. He said, "We thought we would go some morning before he got up." We did so. His housekeeper went and told him who was come to see him. He told her to tell the gentlemen to sit down and he would be with them soon, which she did. He came into the room, just spoke to us, and said to the housekeeper, "Fetch these gentlemen each a glass of rum," and walked forward right through the house and out of door. As he did not return, we began to think he was giving us the slip, so we went to see for him, but could see nothing of him. But there was a barn at a small distance from the house; we thought he must be there and could be nowhere else. We went to the barn, there was a female there; but as we learnt afterwards, he had charged her not to tell, so we could make nothing of her. Nor could we find him. But as we were going away, one of us, looking back, saw him looking through a loophole. We returned back and asked him to come down, as we wanted to have some talk with him about the Chapel. But, whatever we said, we could neither get him to come down off the hay, nor promise anything towards the building of the chapel.

If it had been some land they had wanted to sell or mortgage, Old Holt would soon have been with them. He was constantly after buying or mortgaging land. His income was reported to be about ten thousand pounds per year. He had no children, nor any very near relations. Wm. Turner Esq., of Helmshore, being very friendly with Mr. Holt a short time before his death, Holt made him the residuary legatee in his will. It is said that W.T. got from eighty to ninety thousand pounds; though if a relation at all, very distant. His estates of land (except two which were not in the will), he gave to his relations, estates of land to some worth one thousand pounds per year, and less amounts of land and money to more distant relations.

Once when travelling by the railway to Liverpool, another gentleman who knew Mr. Holt mentioned some of the above doings which I had often heard before. After some conversation, I remarked that after all a miser was a better man to the community than a spendthrift. Another gentleman in the carriage objected and said a spendthrift was a very great deal better than a miser, because he spent his money and circulated it in the country, which did much good. If he was a sportsman, or spent his money in racing or any other pleasure, the money were circulating in the country and there was no comparison between him and the miser. He was doing good while the miser was doing no good. I said such a miser as Holt was not so bad to the community as to himself, but a spendthrift was a very bad man both to the community and himself. Let us just examine these two characters, how they affect the community: (as follows I give my argument, in part, and the ideas on which I founded my argument on that occasion). Holt, who we are now calling a miser, let us examine first. I do not recollect hearing that Holt in all his life, ever gave anything towards any charitable object, or any other thing, no, not so much as a halfpenny to a child, (except once, sixpence to a missionary collector). He broke stones in the road before he would pay anybody to do it. He lived upon coarse food, wore coarse clothing, old cast-off clothes when he could get them. He wasted nothing which he thought would lose him any money, but took care of everything by which he thought he could make any money. The fact is, he consumed for his own body very little of the fruits of other men's labour. He laboured hard to find out who would sell their land cheapest or give the highest rate of interest for a mortgage on land; or what bank would give the best interest for what money he had not spent in land or mortgages. If those persons who will sell their land the cheapest or give the highest rate of interest for money are the most needy persons and if it be a deed of charity to help the most needy first, Holt abounded in this charity, although done from another motive. The fact is, he helped the needy. The money which he had lent on mortgages, or that which he had given for land or the money he had in the bank would all be circulated in the country and perhaps most of it employed, by plodding, laborious commercial men, and men of great minds, studious, scheming men who are constantly inventing one great improvement after another; which is a blessing to the community and so far fulfilling the commandment of God to replenish the earth and subdue it, overcome, it, conquer it, in vegetation, minerals, water, steam, gas, electricity, make all its elements subject to us. God hath given a law to everything He hath made, and hath so ordered it, that a studious, scheming, economical man cannot help being made a blessing to the community whether he doeth it from that motive or not. Holt consumed but little of the production of other men's labour, but circulated his money in the country.

The spendthrift also circulated his money in the country, but let us see how he circulated his money by keeping racehorses, hunting dogs, game preserves, game keepers, and a large quantity of servants to look after these things, he attends all kinds of places of amusements. What are all the people doing on whom he is spending all this money? Why, they are producing nothing but amusement! His racehorses, hunting dogs, game keepers, and all these servants, himself and all what they produce for the community? Why, nothing but famine. His money is all spent in consuming the fruits of the hard labouring people, and upon those men, women and animals which are producing nothing for the good of the community. Human beings, employed right, are worth more than what they consume. Look what has been done since Noah's Flood! What houses, towns and cities have been built! Roads, canals, railways, agriculture, naval and other great works have been accomplished, all of which now are fixed capital. But where is the produce or fixed capital of the money laid out by the spendthrift? Why there is neither fixed nor floating capital. Money spent that way is like a fire consuming all before it leaving nothing behind it but ruin, famine and woeful sorrow.

I have no doubt on my mind but a miser is a better man to the community than a spendthrift, but which of the two is the greater sinner, I cannot tell. The spendthrift is a disorderly busybody, working not at all to produce any good to the community. Paul says that, if any would not work, neither should he eat. The man mentioned in the Gospel who had got plenty to live upon said, "This will I do. I will pull down my barns and build greater, and there will I bestow all my fruits and my goods." And so, he would go out of business, work no more, but would take his ease, eat, drink and be merry. How long did he live afterwards? Not another day.

LOWER MILL 1840

For the last five or six years we have been employing upwards of fifty men, masons, &c, for building. Thanks be to God, no one has been killed, though there has been some narrow escapes. We always charged the men to put up their scaffolding firm, the neglect of which has been the cause of a-many accidents. Let my soul acknowledge God in all His goodness and mercy to us, and to all our workpeople. We now saw, by several things which were taking place, that there would be another commercial panic. We therefore made up our minds that we would stop building, or nearly so, for a time. As there was a Wesleyan Chapel in course of building at Bacup, towards which my brothers and I gave one hundred and fifty pounds, and subscriptions were then making for our new Chapel at Rawtenstall, towards which my brothers and I gave one thousand pounds, and as the building of this Chapel was about to be let, we advised the masons and joiners which we had been employing to take the Chapel to build. In which they succeeded, and towards the close of this year, we commenced spinning in our Rawtenstall Lower Mill. As we had seen the gathering storm, or commercial panic, which would soon overtake us, we did not push machinery fast into our new Mill, but rather held back. Banks were stopping, and mills shutting up every week. We also began to do less business to Canada. We had a great deal of money out in that country, say from thirty to forty thousand pound.

In consequence of the rebellion of 1837 in that country, we had a-many of bad debts. From our experience, it appeared to us morally bad to give long credits in any country. We have often found workpeople whom we have employed who have got involved in debt, have become careless in their work and unmanageable; and

Lower Mill viewed from Holly Mount

who, in consequence of being heavily in debt with shopkeepers in the neighbourhood, have become insolvent and would sooner leave the country than do their work in a proper way. The credit given in Canada for dry goods, were generally six to twelve month, and sometimes more. A-many of such creditors in the time of the rebellion availed themselves of the opportunity and quit the country and left their debts unpaid, which begot in them no desire to return. We lost a great deal of money in Canada through bad debts. In Canada, the grocery and spirit trade were more upon the ready money system.

Mr. Kay, our partner, wanted to go into that trade. We had a particular objection to have anything to do with the selling of wines or spirits. In the beginning of the year 1841, Mr. Kay came over to England. We gave him to understand at that time that we would never go into the spirit trade upon any account whatever. After buying our Spring goods for Canada, but not so many as usual, Mr. Kay returned to Canada, without coming to any agreement whether to dissolve partnership or not. We had come to this conclusion; if Mr. Kay went into the spirit trade, we would have a dissolution of partnership, as we would not have anything to do with the spirit trade, nor be in partnership with anyone who was in that trade.

Our new Chapel was rising very nicely. The builders were getting on well with their work, and we were giving our attention to it; and to the Wesleyan Society, to the Temperance Society, and to the National Anti-Corn Law League. We were holding Free Trade meetings wherever we could. Brother Peter and I worked hard in the Free Trade cause. I used to deliver free trade lectures in railway trains, and I often found ideas which I had thrown out in this way, soon after worked up in the newspapers. This encouraged me to go on, and I have been many times thanked, when I have got out of the carriage, for my lecture.

FREE TRADE

I found some objectors always harping upon reciprocity. They would not take off import duties of goods imported from a foreign country, except that country took off their import duties on goods imported from us. But if this be fully investigated, it will be seen that the country who impose the duty, pay that duty themselves. For instance, take England and America. Suppose England allow the produce of America, say cotton, corn or any of the produce to be imported free, but that the Americans put import duty, say twenty per cent, upon English manufactured goods imported into that country, that duty can injure England no more than what such an imposition may impoverish the Americans, who will have to pay it themselves. For England will just do the same by America as the man who fetches a cartload of coals for a cottage house. He says "I have paid so much for the coals, so much for tolls on the road, and I must have so much for myself, horse and cart," and he charges the whole to the cottager to whom he delivers the coals. So the cottager pays the toll bars, as well as all other expenses.

So it is when a merchant sends goods to America. He puts the duty which they have imposed upon the amount of the goods, and also his profit, and charges the whole to the Americans, which they must pay either in gold or with their produce. If in gold, most likely the merchant will exchange it for a bill on England, to someone who has bought American produce, and sent it to England to meet those Bills of exchange. For no country can absolutely pay with gold, nor could any country sell their produce for gold absolutely. If England could do it, she would soon have all the gold in the world; but before she could accomplish that the inhabitants would be famished to death for they could not eat the gold, it is in itself neither meat nor clothing. Therefore all trade is barter. The Americans must take the English produce, or the English cannot take their produce. Merchants must have a profit on the aggregate, or they cannot continue trade. Therefore, it would follow that the

Americans must take as many goods from England with the twenty per cent duty, as if there were no duty at all. The evil will fall upon the Americans themselves, and not upon England. The Americans who produce exportable produce will have to pay the tax imposed on import produce, which tax will flow into the hands of these Americans who produce such kind of produce as the tax is imposed upon; and instead of it being an injury to England, it would be rather in its favour. Because the American manufacturers being protected would be a means for them to rest upon, and eventually less able to compete with English manufacturers in other parts of the world.

So class legislation damages its own country and is its own tormentor. Reciprocity laws are like the government of one country agreeing with the government of another country, how much each government must rob one class of its own subjects to protect or give to another class. Or, in other words, robbing the working bees of their honey to feed the drones. So when I was travelling by the railway and met with objectors to free trade, I used to meet their objections by throwing as much light as I could upon the evil of class legislation, both as regards the moral and commercial world. As trade was then very bad, I often got attentive hearers.

HIGHER MILL FIRE

The distress in manufacturing districts were very great, many mills shut up, and a great number working short time. And when the distress was about at its height say October 30th 1841, Sunday, (the very day that the Tower of London was burnt down), early this morning, there came a most tremendous rapping at our door, Holly Mount, and a shout, "The mill's on fire!" I jumped out of bed and looked through the window, and saw our Higher Mill was on fire. I dressed myself and went to the mill. A water engine was soon got to the place, and another two arrived soon after. And with other assistance they saved the steam engine and the warehouse, and a part of the machinery, but the mill was burnt down. How this Mill took fire, we never could ascertain, it was wrapped up in mystery to us, for we had no lights in the Mill on the previous night. The fire first broke out in the dressing room, which appeared to us the most unlikely place in the Mill. Another thing was strange to us: a neighbour discovered the fire before our watchman, whom we kept mostly on purpose to watch against fire, and who could not give us a satisfactory account why he did not discover the fire the first. It was a mysterious thing to us, but God might permit this fire to take place for some wise end which we know not, for I am sure nothing takes place without His knowledge.

Our workpeople worked hard in putting out the fire, and to save all the property they possibly could. We had a large stock of goods in the warehouse, all of which they got out and took down to the Lower Mill. We were insured, but not to the amount of damage as per valuation, by several thousands of pounds. But the loss to the people was very great at a time like this, when trade was so bad, so many mills shut up, others working short time. We had very heavy stocks of goods, and could not sell, and did not know how to go on to make more without loss and accumulation of our stocks. But we saw our workpeople were in a most pitiable situation, so we made our minds as to get some more machinery into the Lower Mill, and get our workpeople into work again as soon as we could; which we accomplished in a short time.

LETTERS TO JONATHAN

My wife felt a great interest in the welfare of the people, particularly to the females. She had now three Wesleyan Classes of females, having been this year appointed to her Tuesday Class in addition to her Thursday and Sunday Classes. She laboured hard amongst them, and felt her charge. Shrewsbury was then our Minister, being appointed at the last Conference. He was a man of good sense, a clear head, a faithful Minister, a truly enlightened conscience, a very good preacher of our Lord Jesus Christ, a good pious man, his equal rarely to be met with. I have at different times had sweet conversation with him on religious subjects, church and state, and on politics and free trade. He had a mind like a deep well, which could give out and take in. We could not always see the same, but the more we entered into the subjects on which we conversed, and the nearer we came to each other in our views. He was much beloved by all the families of Holly Mount. My son Jonathan was gone to America where he continued to live all the three years. Mr. Shrewsbury remained at Rawtenstall, who Mr. Shrewsbury did not forget to remember when engaged in prayer in our family. I will give here copies of a few letters to Jonathan.

Holly Mount, June 28th 1841

My dear Son,

As your dear Mother had given all the news worth naming I may at once dispense with that and say I had much satisfaction in reading your letter of May 13th which duly came to hand. I feel great pleasure in writing a few lines to you, and more so because I am not only writing to my child but to a child of God, and first I would say, be sure to know every day that you do enjoy the witness of the spirit to bear witness with yours that you are the Lord's. In order to maintain this constantly pray that God may implant truth within your heart, and strive as much as possible to practice the same. Second, be diligent in your business, endeavour to make yourself fully master of it, and when not engaged in your merchandise, waste not your time with the customs and fashions of the place, but be diligent to improve your mind with all useful knowledge. I know you are a good one at foregoing any thing that you know is only a phantom or what we may call wasting time in nonsense, if you only just give yourself to think, I know you will forego every thing of that kind. If you pay attention to the above, you will make yourself what I call a straight forward clever man, which I have no doubt you have made up your mind so to do. Then pray to God for his assistance, and let nothing upon earth turn you aside. I have not much time to write to you, but my heart is with you and is very warm and happy, and I feel a breathing up to God for you; we have hard times here Jonathan, say, what we call bad times. But if faithful to God I have no doubt but he will bring us through, pray for us, and let us all pray that we may be made a blessing in the earth. I have been of opinion for a long time, that merchants and manufacturers may be instrumental if faithful in the hands of God of the greatest means of human happiness and the evangelisation of the whole world, turn that over in your mind, and when you have time give me your thoughts upon the subject. Merchants have a great influence, then let that be turned into a righteous channel and what will it do. Manufacturers have a great influence too, and they may be useful towards the conversion of great numbers of the poor, may God help us to my to do all the good we can while me live. I think I must now stop till I have had your thoughts.

I am my dear Son,
Your very affectionate Father
David Whitehead

To Jonathan Wood Whitehead
Montreal, Canada.

Holly Mount, Sept. 2nd 1841

My Dear Jonathan,

Your favour of Augt. 12th came to hand on the 30 Idem just two days before your Mother left Holly Mount for Maidstone with your Uncle and Aunt Kay (they would go through London). She left us in good health and was very glad to hear from you, and as well as myself highly pleased with your letter, I am glad to see you take a proper and correct view of the plan tradesmen should take both as regards their prudence in business and their moral influence in the world, but where you state, "had mercantile men acted with prudence and caution for the last 2 or 3 years," instead of 2 or 3 years, you should have said 8 or 9 years. It was about that time when the Bank of England and other banks began to be so extravagant in the issue of Bank notes, and liberal in discounts, and tradesmen were so foolish as to avail themselves of the offer and have thereby been caught in the snare. Paper money is a dangerous thing, it is false money. Thousands have been ruined by it, it is like a bubble, and if it give way when men are depending upon it, down they tumble. How often do we see tradesmen, through a desire to be rich, or for the love of money which, as St Paul says, is "the root of all evil," get upon this rotten foundation. Bill drawing, and ruin is sure to come; no tradesmen ought ever to draw a Bill but for value received, and no wise and sound tradesman will ever suffer himself to be drawn upon. He that suffers it is the borrower, and as the wise man says, must be servant to the lender. A wise tradesman will never go beyond his capital. He may not get money as fast as other men for a time, but he is making his ground good; and every wise tradesman, warrior or builder must make his ground good as he goes on, or he will never accomplish any great work. The Corn Laws or any other monopolies are very bad for trade and particularly so for the poor, I am inclined to think that the greatest evil is men going beyond their capital, and that there will be a most awful reckoning on the judgment day upon this account. Many thousands of poor people are now distressed and dying for want of work and food, partly on account of themselves running into debt when times were better, but mostly through the wickedness of tradesmen going beyond their capital, which wickedness along with the Corn Laws and other monopolies arises out of the love of money which is the root of all evil. I pray that God may make you into a wise tradesman, and I desire you to examine all the bearings of these things, and see if you cannot find out what is the cause of all this evil. You may say at once, sin, and the cure would be to have all men converted, True but how is it that religious people and some say good men fail and pay five or ten shillings in the pound, and how often do we hear religious people soften it down and say they have been imprudent, Would it not be more proper to say they have been wicked or downright wicked? A good tradesman should never desire to be rich – a wise one never will – but should do all he can honestly with his own capital to get all the money he can; a wise one certainly will. The next thing is to use the money when got in the best way, as he must give an account in the last day. A part must be devoted to religious purposes. How much it must be decided by his own judgement. The whole of the rest should be used for charitable and useful purposes. Trade is useful, and to put a man into the way of procuring his own living, educating and enlightening the poor ignorant people, and to give labouring men. All this is being charitable. A tradesman should extend his trade as he increases in capital, but no farther; or I cannot see how he can justify himself, except he sees some other way in which he can become more useful to the community, for he that won't work ought not to eat. A tradesman should do all with a single eye to the glory of God. By so doing he will be able to do much good, and there is a pleasure in doing good when we have a heart to do it. Therefore, Jonathan, be "diligent in business and fervent in spirit, serving the Lord." I have given you in this letter a few outlines for a tradesman, the details of which I leave for you to work out, and I should like you to be a tradesman of the right kind. I pray that God may direct and bless you in all you do. I am glad to hear that you still like a book, but as I have told you before, reading men's works is something like looking at fine buildings – it is useful in a proper way. You know we must procure some tools for ourselves or we shall never be able to build. With love,

>   I am my dear Jonathan
>   Your affectionate Father
>   David Whitehead

To Jonathan Whitehead
Montreal, Canada

NB to explain myself better, by book reading and study we gain knowledge which is our duty, but to be always gaining knowledge without employing it is like a man procuring tools for building but never begins to build. Employ knowledge when obtained and it will grow healthy and strong. D.W.

>   Holly Mount, Rawtenstall,
>   1 Decbr, 1841.

Dear Jonathan,

Your favour of Oct. 28th came to hand on the 16th Novr., of which I shall notice before I conclude. As I know you like a sermon, I have enclosed one, preached by our old friend Jacob Grimshaw. I heard him preach it in the Longholme Chapel. He has also preached it at Bacup, Newchurch and Rakefoot. I think there were a desire from all the places to have it printed. The creation of this sermon was through a sermon being in the neighbourhood and written by the Rev. S. Whitaker, son of the late Samuel Whitaker of Newchurch, in which sermon he broadly asserts that no one living in England can be saved out of the established Church of England. In fact, it is Pusyism in its strangest form, which is spreading very much in the established Church in this neighbourhood. When your mother has been soliciting subscriptions for our chapel, several of the church people has told her that they believe us to be heretics, and could not in their conscience give anything towards building a Methodist Chapel. This was from some of the highest Tories in the country. Jonathan, I like Tories no better than ever I did. Dr Clark was a Whig in politics, and I think every thorough-thinking wise and good man must be one. I should like you to take up no side in politics till you finally understand them, of which you will be able if you study truth and equity between Kingdom and Kingdom, or nation and nation, and what is right betwixt man and man in the sight of God, or according to the word of God.

Radicalism so called is as bad as Toryism; they meet in their extremes and are both tyrannical. A wise and good man likes laws made equitable and strong, and kept when made. Nor will he break the laws of his country to mend a bad one, say such as are oppressive to the poor, but will try lawfully to get them put right. Righteousness is what we should all aim at, and I pray that God may enable you to strive for it in all things.

You wrote in your letter of Aug. 12th that when winter sets in you intend to commence the learning of the French language. You say there are two ways: "1st taking lessons from a French teacher, 2nd. boarding in the country with French people, where nothing but the French language is spoken." I will leave you in this matter to use your own judgement, and hope you will hit upon the plan which will be the most expeditious. Your mother and I (as well as your sisters) perused over your last letter with great interest and I feel glad that you are not reading superficially, and I hope thereby you will procure tools with which you will hereafter work. Certainly there are two ways: 1st. we may look at other men's work to please our senses, 2nd. to improve our mind. The latter way I hope you will adhere to. I also see you are after buying more books. I would buy no books but such as are useful, and when you have got what is useful out of them, sell them again. By so doing you will not invest much more money.

Nothing gives me greater satisfaction than to hear that you take great pleasure in reading the scriptures and private prayer. Reading the scriptures in the way you state is profitable, and as you say,"every word has meaning." Jonathan still prize that Book; it is the Book in which God is speaking to his creature. In it we are instructed how to pray; and prayer is power with God when offered through his all prevalent son. Therefore be sure to keep up private prayer, and commit your way to God who is able and willing to direct you in all things both in this world and that which is to come. The concluding part of your letter, "My only desire is to please God" gives us a full view of the state of your mind, and I must say you are right. Go on, mind the same things and may the God of Abraham bless you.

Your mother in her last letter to you would inform you of our old Mill being burnt down. Towards this loss we hope to get from the Fire Office £4,471.19.0. Though our loss is great, yet how much more so for the poor workpeople. They are very badly off. Last week Thomas Heaton of Balladenbrook called his creditors together. He owed about £2,600, and had nothing or but little to offer to them except his machinery. His landlord wants £400 for rent, and I do not think his machinery will sell for it at present. So Balladenbrook will be a most distressing case for the people there; but after all I feel thankful that God is my portion. I feel a trusting in him. My dear son, whatever else, live near to God; and I hope at last to meet all my children at the right hand of God, which may He grant for Christ's sake. I close my letter with haste. Your Mother and children join me in love. We are all well.

>I am my dear Jonathan
>Your affectionate Father,
>David Whitehead

To Jonathan Whitehead
Montreal, Canada

Brothers and I joined the Anti-Corn Law League from a thorough conviction that free trade was a great movement in the right direction to help the Ark of God, as it appeared to us impossible for war and bloodshed ever to cease while we had such an abominable system of class legislation. We viewed the Corn Law as the keystone of the arch of tyrannical monopoly, which stone, we thought, if once drawn, would be a fine introduction to free trade in this country, and would have its effect through all the world. It would tend very much to establishing universal peace and hasten the "millennium", "when war and bloodshed shall come to end, and righteousness and peace be established in the earth."

Therefore we did all we could to enlighten the public upon this great movement. It was a great pleasure to give part of our time and money towards hastening it on. In the year 1842, January 29, we gave thirty pounds to the Anti-Corn Law League. We had several delightful conversations with Mr. Shrewsbury upon this subject, who was willing to help any movement which would tend towards the coming of the Kingdom of Christ. But he was one who would not run in the dark or mist, which we were anxious to clear away. He was eventually convinced of the righteousness of our cause, and wrote a pamphlet, "Christian thoughts on Free Trade, in a letter to Thomas, Peter and David Whitehead."

Our new chapel was now nearly ready for opening, but as William Cooke Taylor LL.D said in his "Notes of a tour in the Manufacturing Districts of Lancashire, in a series of Letters to His Grace the Archbishop of Dublin",[6] when speaking of the children of Holly Mount, Rawtenstall, in the Forest of Rossendale "though stags are banished from the Forest, it has still a large and fine assortment of pretty little dears!" Now I think I must not omit giving the names of these "pretty little dears", and their subscriptions towards our new Wesleyan Chapel, which were as follows:

Jonathan Wood Whitehead	£10. 0. 0
Thomas Hoyle Whitehead	3. 0. 0
Ann Whitehead	4. 4. 0
Elizabeth Whitehead	5. 5. 0
Sarah Whitehead	2.10.6
Mary Whitehead	2. 2. 0
John Ormerod Whitehead	2. 2. 6
Samuel Sanderson Whitehead	2. 2. 0
David Whitehead, Jnr.	2. 2. 0
Thomas Hoyle Whitehead and James Ormerod Whitehead, Hen and chickens	18. 4
Thomas Whitehead, Jnr.	10.10. 0
Joseph Wood Whitehead	10.10. 0
Alice Whitehead	4. 4. 0
David Greenwood Whitehead	2.10. 0

Longholme Methodist Chapel, Rawtenstall

Peter Halstead Whitehead	2.10.0
John Blakey Whitehead	10.10.0
Marianne Whitehead	4.0.0
Peter Ormerod Whitehead	2.10.0
Elizabeth Whitehead	2.5.0
Margaret Whitehead	2.5.0
Thomas Kay Whitehead	2.0.0

The above subscriptions were given towards the new Wesleyan Chapel, Longholme, Rawtenstall. which was opened on Friday, March 18, 1842, by the Rev. J. Dixon, President of the Conference. Collections of the various services on the occasion were £397.8.5½.

THE PLUG DRAWING RIOTS

When the day arrived they commenced (in the month of August, 1842); the plan they adopted was to draw the plug, that is to draw the water out of each steam boiler, but not to break any machinery. In this way the people assembled together in great quantities and visited the mills, one after another, and drew, or caused to be drawn, the plug of each steam boiler. In country places they dispatched smaller numbers to do the work. A small number came to our mill, but our engineer being a stout, sturdy kind of man, asked them what they wanted. They said, "To draw the plug." "Nay", he said, "You shall draw no plug. I will have a better show than you make, or you shall draw no plug here." They said, "Well, then, we will fetch them," meaning the mob, who were at another mill in the neighbourhood.

So they brought the whole mob. When they came, the engineer said, "You cannot draw the plug, you cannot find it, but I will draw it for you." He drew the plug and they all went quietly away, without doing any damage whatever.

Trade being bad at the time, of course we were quite willing for the works to stand as long as the people were wishful. We were asked if we would have soldiers, and we said, no, we would have nothing of the kind, but would stop as long as the people wished us. As far as I could learn, the whole of the mills were stopped in this way, and great terror and fear appeared to be in some parts of the country, but they could not draw the Anti-Corn Law League into the plot. But hundreds of the League were sworn in Special Constables. These men were for peace and their plan was to protect property, and to have no class legislation, but free trade. So the Tory Protectionists could not catch the Anti-Corn Law League in their class trap.

ANTI-CORN LAW LEAGUE

This year [1842] was a year of great trial for manufacturers and much suffering for the workpeople. But through the Anti-Corn Law League holding meetings in various parts of Lancashire and Yorkshire, the minds of the workpeople were enlightened, so they saw clearly that the cause of their distress was not on account of the improvement of machinery. One cause was short crops, then speculation with false capital and over-trading. Another great cause [was] bad legislation – taxing corn, sugar and other food, not for revenue, but for a Class. The people were told, and a-many attended to the advice, that they should also learn economy and save a little money instead of spending it on drink; and qualify themselves by buying forty-shilling freeholds to enable them to send men to Parliament who would go against class legislation. They were also given to understand that it often happened, when there were a short crop in one country, that there were a good crop in another country, and that free trade would allow us to exchange the surplus produce of our manufactures for their surplus produce of food; or, in other words, allow us to sell in the dearest markets and buy in the cheapest.

The Tory Protectionists, with a view to catch in their Class trap the Anti-Corn Law League, resorted to their old trick; sent out their emissaries who pretended to be Chartist, and held Sunday meetings on the moors or on the tops of the hills, and made speeches to the ignorant people who attended, advising them to stop all the mills in England, to commence on a certain day, and continue their work until they had stopped the whole.

Rawtenstall,
16th November, 1843.

Dear Jonathan,

Our last to you was on the 3rd. inst., and your favour of the 28th October came to hand yesterday. You will see by our last of the 3rd inst. that we have no wish for you to establish a business in Canada unless you would think it would be better to do so. If you leave Canada, how soon could we get the money out of that concern? Because what can we do with all the young folks without some money to set them agoing.

There is a fear of them doing worse than a little business, viz. none at all if our money be first in Canada, but we think you rather misunderstand us about beginning a little business or we misunderstand you about your trudging along in a little way all your life &c., &c. Now my idea in beginning business in a little way is this: if I wanted a young plant to grow into a fine tree I would plant it in a snug corner where it would not be much seen or known until it has got its roots firmly held to the ground. Then it would begin to grow up and spread its branches and be noticed as a goodly tree, and would be able to stand the winters. So of commerce, apply the figure; it is a good one and one which is applicable to the richest and greatest mercantile house in England. We are quite sure it is the best way to begin business in this country in a small and quiet way until they have got so grounded in it that it begins to spread and grow [so] that opposition has no chance of running it down, its roots having got so deep hold of commerce before its opponents were aware that it was of any note. We will wait for your news, but we are anxiously expecting some good remittances. If we do not get a good deal of money from Canada, it will do badly for us. Give us all the information you can about the affairs of the concern, we seem to be quite in a mist about it. We want about £11,000 to pay off Stott and Smith and ourselves. This we considered a deal of money. Could you or Mr. Kay give us any idea when the above sum could be remitted? as we shall want the above before we begin to receive any of the profits of

the concern. If we cannot get it, how can we extend our business, so as to keep all our lads at work? We want you to understand that perfectly, and look into it as well as you can, because if we had the money we could tell better what to do. Perhaps you will see our letter to Kay, Whitehead and Co., which will show. We want what money possibly can be remitted. We are all well. D. W.
   Yours very affectionately,
     Thomas Whitehead and Brothers.
To Jonathan Wood Whitehead
Canada.

            Holly Mount,
            Jany. 27th 1844

My Dear Jonathan,

My last to you was Jany $3^{rd}/44$ since which I have received none from you; in my last I had not time to do more than just to allude to one passage in your letter of Decr $11^{th}/43$ which letter, with the exception of the passage alluded to, I think is a sensible letter; but now let me tell you once for all (although my former advice I think has always been to the same effect) that I wish all my children to do in this world what God intends them to do; not to miss their providential way, which I am sure they will not if they live near to God in prayer and fully commit their care to him.

 Getting money, or what business they may follow, is the last consideration with me, only that it be what God intends it to be. The first thing is, seek the kingdom of God and its righteousness; then to be diligent in the business to which God has called them; to do everything in the best way and at the time it should be done, in the same way as a good farmer would plough his field at the best time and the best way, get his seed in when the weather was most favourable, after fencing, weeding, and all other necessary work; then he has taken all the care that belongs to him, whether it is a good crop or a bad one, with that he has nothing to do, nor has he a right to care, nor has a tradesman any right to care whether he gets much money or little, it is whether he is doing what God would have him to do, and whether he is doing to the best of his judgement in every thing in the calling to which God hath appointed him; that is his care. I wish you to take care of all my letters to you for I have written them with a desire for your future good, and I think if you notice them they will be useful where ever your lot may be cast, and whatever your calling may be. To conclude, Jonathan tell me, do you enjoy the witness of the Spirit to bear witness with yours that you are a child of God, are you regular in the attendance of your class, do not forget to answer me these questions.

I remain your affectionate Father
David Whitehead

To Jonathan Wood Whitehead
Montreal, Canada

Eventually it was agreed for Jonathan to return home, and Mr. Kay to wind up the concern. Though Mr. Kay had begun business for himself or entered into partnership with another person who was in the grocery and spirit trade, we thought he would be best able to wind up the above concern, having from the beginning been connected with it, and as it would have been difficult for anyone to wind it up without his assistance. I had spent more than ten years in trying to establish that concern in which it had a great part of my time, in the course of which time there were so many bad debts that there were very little, if any, profit made. Mr. Kay was dissatisfied (though he had the management of the sale of the goods) and wanted to do something else.

I am quite satisfied that it will take ten years to establish a mercantile house of that kind upon sound principles before much if any, profit, can be made. To establish a house like the one referred to, on sound principles, would be to establish public confidence, both here and in Canada, can only be acquired by uprightness, punctuality and time. After being at it so long and then to give it up, is something like a man beginning to build a house for himself to live in; after being at this work for years, fancies he should like to have another kind of house to that which he is building. Therefore he abandons it, and begins to build another; in this way he may go on all his lifelong, always dissatisfied. It was the greatest dissatisfaction I ever met with in all my life, to begin the business before referred to, and not to continue it. I consider so much of my time completely thrown away.

I would advise all young men never to go into business with a desire to get rich, and to take care never to go into partnership with one who is anxious to be rich; but go into that business at which they would like best to work, then be diligent, upright and honest, never tell a lie, and do the best you can in all you have to do in your business. Never mind whether you get rich or not: leave that to God. Then you will have pleasure in your business all your life long, whether you be rich or poor. Few of this kind of people will ever be poor. God always helps the man that tries to help himself.

I believe I am in the business in which God intended I should be. I always feel happy when I do my business in the best way I know, whether it turn out profitable or otherwise, same as the farmer ought to be when he takes care to get his seed in the field at the most favourable time, whether it be a good crop or otherwise. No wise man will ever desire to be rich; a truly good man can have no such desire.

Our [cotton] broker, Mr. E. Unsworth of Liverpool, related to me the following circumstance, viz: A farmer's son from some of the southern counties, who had procured about £17 and had made up his mind to emigrate to America, came to Liverpool a few days ago and agreed for his passage in a certain vessel to America. He took up his lodgings until the vessel should sail at the same Inn where I dined nearly every day. This emigrant, who was dressed in fustian clothes, being one day standing at a shop window, a stranger, a young man who was also dressed in fustian, stepped up to him and said, "Are you going to America?" The emigrant said, "Yes." "So am I stranger. What vessel are you going by?" [The] Emigrant stranger named the vessel. "I am going by the same vessel. How glad I am that I have met with you! We shall be such fine company. Come, let us go and look at the vessel." [The] emigrant had no objections, so they went down to the docks and looked at the vessel. After which they continued to walk about the docks for some time and coming up to a public house, the stranger said

"Come, let us go in and have each a gill." Just after they had got in and each had a gill of beer, comes in another man, only middlingly dressed. He pulled out of his pocket a handful of notes, laid them upon the table and said "Now, my lads! I am a cotton weaver and have just drawn my fortune. Last night I was playing with some soldiers, and I'll tell you how we did: we put down five pounds at a time, and I put a halfpenny under a jug. If they guessed, they took all up, and if not, I took all up: and now I'll play with you if you like." The stranger played with him for five pounds and won. He played again and won again who whispered to the emigrant and said "The old fool will lose all his money, you might as well have some of it. Will you try?" The emigrant tried five pounds and lost it; he tried another five pounds and lost that. He tried five pounds more, and lost that also. The stranger got up and walked out, then the man with whom he had been playing, and who had got his money, also walked out, and left the emigrant alone; who only just then came to his senses, and saw he had been swindled out of his money. He came to the Inn in great distress; the company took pity upon the young man, made a collection for him and paid his fare by the vessel to America. Mr. Unsworth said to me, "I was very sorry for the young man, and did what I could to get him a little money to help him out of his difficulties, for, about thirty years ago, soon after I came to Liverpool:

"One fine day, when walking about the docks and watching the vessels come in, a country looking man about my own age entered into conversation with me in a very friendly way. We walked about for a considerable time. Eventually we passed a woman selling shrimps, of whom he bought a gill and said to me, 'Come, let us go into this public house, and have each a gill of porter and eat these shrimps.' The day being hot, and I felt a little tired, agreed to his proposal at once. We had no sooner got our porter, and sat down to eat the shrimps, but in comes an aged man, pulled out of his pocket a handful of banknotes, threw them upon the table and said, 'Now, my lads! I am a cotton weaver, and have just drawn my fortune. Last night I was playing wid [with] some soldiers and I'll tell you how we did: we put down five pounds at a time, and put a halfpenny under a jug. If they guessed, they took all up, if not, I took all up. Now I'll play wid you if you like.' "So the man who had been so friendly with me played with the old man for five pounds and won. He played again and won again. He whispered to me and said the old fool will lose all his money! 'You might as well have some of it. Will you try?' I said, 'No, I will have none of his money; if I found it in the street I would give it back to the old man.'

"Shortly he got up and walked out, then the old man got up and walked out, and left me alone in the room. I said to myself, 'Lord have mercy on me! This was a trap, and how easily I might have been caught.' For until they had both left the room it had never entered into my mind that they had any intention to swindle me out of my money."

This is a fine lesson for wild speculators. I have often related the above narrative in order to show the moral lesson which I think is striking and very good. Mr. Unsworth wanted to have no money but such as he might obtain honourably and lawfully: in consequence of which he could not be drawn into the snare. But the emigrant was anxious to get money even by dishonourable means, and therefore easy to entrap. "They that will be rich fall into temptation and a snare." How true. And again "He that maketh haste to be rich shall not be innocent or unpunished." "Wealth gotten by vanity shall be diminished, but he that gathereth by labour shall increase."

And therefore I would advise all young men never to go into business with a desire to get rich, and to take care never to go into partnership with anyone who is anxious to be rich. Such anxiety is a tyrant to the possessor, and an evil to those who are connected with such. Riches, wealth, or money are all good in themselves. They are good things of the "earth" which "is the Lord's and the fullness thereof" and to them to whom they are entrusted carry a heavy responsibility. They are good to be used righteously but not to set an inordinate attachment upon them, "for the love of money is the root of all evil."

NEW LONGHOLME CHAPEL

On Friday April 4th 1845, we had the opening of the organ of our Wesleyan Chapel, Longholme, Rawtenstall. The collections of this day and the Sunday following were £324.18.10¾. The expenses incurred in erecting the new organ and painting the Chapel amounted to £610.8.2. Subscriptions, with the above collections (towards which brothers and I gave upwards of £360), amounted to £700.19.6., leaving a balance over the above expenses of £90.11.4, which went towards lessening the debt of the Chapel.

This Chapel and organ including the ground cost upwards of £6,300, It is a good, plain, substantial and comfortable Chapel, and will seat about 1,300 people. This Chapel, and the old Chapel (now a school), and the preacher's house, say all the premises together, cost upwards of £8,300.

It might appear to some that Longholme, as the Chapel bears that name though built at Rawtenstall, was the place where Methodism first commenced in this neighbourhood. But this was not the case. A Wesleyan Class Meeting was established at Rawtenstall long before Longholme became any place of note. I can recollect going through Longholme myself when it was a field of thistles, and not a building upon it. Rawtenstall was then a small place, and Methodism did not increase much until manufactories began to rise. James Ashworth built a mill for the manufacture of woollen, which mill after a short time was burnt down. After which, Mr. Thomas Kay of Burnley bought and rebuilt the mill for the manufacture of cotton. He also built several cottage houses. In the year 1813, James Moorehouse came to this place, Longholme, and commenced a Methodist Class Meeting. There were then only this Class Meeting, and one Class Meeting at Rawtenstall, in this neighbourhood and from that time to this, Methodism say in the space of 32 years has increased so much as to require the before mentioned premises.

We may say, "What God hath wrought, Glory be to His name!" But to give a just view of the case, we should state that through the increase of manufactories, a-many of Wesleyan Methodists have come from other country places and towns into this neighbourhood, though a great number of members have been raised out of the Sunday School. I believe one reason why is the schoolchildren have been brought to divine service, both on Sunday mornings and in the afternoons, for which I was always a strong advocate. But soon after this time I had to make a most determined stand against our Sunday School Committee. I was informed that they were intending to make a change in the school, viz: to teach in the school in the time of the afternoon service, and that they would send the larger scholars to service in the afternoon, but would retain the smaller scholars in the school as they said they could do the younger scholars more good in religious instruction than they could by hearing a sermon in the Chapel.

I informed the Committee by one of their members that if they adopted that plan, I could not give any more support to that school, nor could I, under such regulations, allow any of my children to teach in it any more. He said the younger scholars could not understand sermons, and he had no doubt but they could talk to the children in such a way as they would understand them better, and would get more good than by hearing sermons. I said that was a great error. It is all well enough, to bring down every subject to the understanding of children when at school, but not in the time of divine service in the Chapel. This would be to teach the children to believe that something better may be done than attending upon divine worship. The preaching of the gospel is a divine appointment, and to teach the children not to attend to it is a sin. "Train up a child in the way he should go, and when he is old he will not depart from it." Form in a child good habits.

For instance, I have one chair in which I generally sit when at home, which I call "my chair"; and I have got such a habit of sitting in it that no other chair is like to me, in fact, out of it I do not feel properly at home. Often, when a friend has called upon me, I have invited him to take the chair in which I usually sit, although there may be another just beside it equally as good, and no doubt my friend would just as soon have it as my chair. But through habit, I happen to think just at the time, my chair is the best, and therefore invite my friend to take it. Then, if habit be so powerful, how necessary to form correct and good habits.

When the children have got the habit of attending the preaching of God's Holy Word, if they are not converted while at school, there is some chance afterwards. But if they are made [to] believe to hear the Word of God is only a secondary thing which can be left to a convenient time with a good conscience, what may we expect? Remember, "Conscience is the faculty of judging of our actions, whether they be good or evil; the determination of the mind with respect to the quality of any action; the knowledge of our own thoughts." So if the children by forcible power of habit can be made to believe that to hear the preaching of God's holy word is only a secondary thing, is it anything strange that they can with a good conscience omit it till a convenient time offer itself?

I think another error which Sunday School teachers make is in thinking that children cannot understand sermons. I will mention a circumstance respecting one child of my own family, viz: one Sunday, having all my family at Chapel, I observed, while the Minister was preaching, one of my sons about twelve years old, who appeared to be very inattentive, trifling with a book in his hand, drawing his finger across the book back as if he might be drawing lines upon it; and then turning the book and drawing diagonal lines upon the book back. I thought I would give him a look of disapprobation, but could not catch his eye, as he held his head rather down, continuing to draw his finger slowly over the book. So I thought I would have some talk with him about it at home. When we got home, I said, "Jonathan, where was the text this morning?" He told me the text, and repeated the words. I said, "Can you give me the heads of the sermon?" He gave me the heads. I said, "Go on and tell me as much of the sermon as you can." He gave me the subdivisions and nearly the whole of the sermon. I found he had brought the sermon home, though I thought he was trifling and paying no attention to the preacher. I said nothing to him about the book and the drawing of his finger over it, as it perhaps might be only his mental power which had set his physical power in motion to assist him in taking in the sermon. If I at any time said to that boy, "Go and hear such a preacher and bring me the sermon," he would go and bring me nearly the whole of the sermon.

Now if there was one child in my family who could do this, how many children may there be of similar minds in a school like ours, of six or seven hundred children? Then away with that opinion, that children cannot understand sermons!

The Committee passed a resolution to try the plan for six weeks, viz: to teach the school in the time of the afternoon service, and to send to Chapel only the larger scholars. So, as I had told them, I would not allow any of my children to teach in the school, and that, if they continued the plan, I had made up my mind to withdraw all my support from the school.

But I was informed after they had tried the plan for a few weeks, a many of the teachers and scholars also did not like it. In fact, the habit of going to the afternoon service had been formed, and they did not feel just at home in that way. I had said a good deal upon the subject, and I believe some of the parents of the children did not like the plan. It is natural for parents who attend the Chapel to like to see their children there; and when parents know that their children will be at the Chapel, it is an inducement for the parents to attend also.

I was very thankful to learn at the end of the six weeks that the plan was given up, and they had again returned to their old plan of bringing all the scholars to divine service both morning and in the afternoon. I am fully convinced that any religious society or church, who keep the children in their school at the time they hold their divine service will not prosper as they would do if they closed their school in the time of their divine worship and brought the schoolchildren to hear the Word of God preached.

The good or bad effects of a good or bad formation of habits in the rising generation tell most powerfully in the course of twenty years. The Temperance Society is doing much good in this neighbourhood which is another good habit, to become a total abstainer from all intoxicating drinks. There is then a greater chance for mental improvement, by which the people will be better able to judge what reforms are most needed for the good of human society. An enlightened people will have enlightened and liberal legislators.

ANTI-CORN LAW LEAGUE

The Anti-Corn Law League have, for a few years, been enlightening the people and educating them so that they may better understand their political rights, and that they may understand the word "Protection". It is a pretty word, and a good word too, when rightly applied. But when one class of men have got an Act of Parliament that they can legally rob another class of men, and when the men who have been robbed want the Act to be repealed, they, the robbers, call out for "Protection!" They do not like to be called robbers, so they call themselves "Protectionists".

Towards the close of this year, the Free Trade agitation came to its climax. At a meeting of the League in Manchester, at which my brothers and I were present, it was agreed to raise £500,000 to carry on the agitation, the subscribers to be called upon for 20 per cent of their subscription at a time, till all was paid if needed. We gave in our names for £500, and in the following year, say 1846, February 3rd we paid our first call of the above subscription, which happened to be also our last call of 20 per cent, viz: £100 to the Anti-Corn Law League; for this year the League gained a triumphant victory, which I had the honour to witness in the House of Lords. The reason for me being in London at the time occurred in the following way. At a meeting of Commissioners of the Rochdale and Burnley Road, it was found that the directors of the railway were going to make some encroachments upon the road. I was deputed to be one of a deputation to London, to try to get such alterations introduced into their Bill, before it passed the House of Parliament, as might satisfy the Commissioners. I think we were to be in London on the 21st of June, and the passing of the Bill for the repeal of the Corn Law, took place on the 25th of June in the House of Lords. The same night, I said to my friends, "I shall go to the House of Lords tonight to hear the Bill passed for the repeal of the Corn Laws." One of my friends said it would be impossible for me to get into the house, for he had been trying to get a note of admittance, but could not get one on any account. I said, "I have no doubt at all but I shall get into the House, and stop there till the Bill is passed." It was his opinion that I should find myself very much mistaken.

I went to the House and found in the lobby Mr. Wilson and three or four Members of Parliament. I told them they must take me into the House of Lords. They said, "Well, we must try!" So I got between two Members of Parliament and we walked into the House. The doorkeeper said nothing to me when we passed him. I wanted particular to hear the Duke of Wellington make his speech, and after being in the House about six or seven hours, and hearing great number of speeches, the old Duke rose and spoke, slow but in a most decisive manner. I stood beside Mr. Wilson who said, "The old Duke is stuffing it into them!"

He [the Duke] told the House that as the other two branches of legislation had agreed to the Bill, they were powerless. Soon after his speech, the business was brought to a close, and as the words "that this Bill do pass" fell from the lips of the Lord Chancellor, a suppressed cheer ran through the ranks of the Free Traders, which was most enthusiastically responded to on the outside of the House. And when Mr. Wilson, Mr. Paulton and I were walking together about five o'clock in the morning from the House of Lords to the League House, people in all directions were shouting "Huzza!" some in cabs twirling their hats out of the cab windows, shouting "Huzza! huzzah!" Mr. Paulton often repeated while on our way and after we got into the house, "Oh! How I should like to shout!" He was so glad, as we all were, of the triumphant victory.

I had to attend a meeting at seven o'clock the same morning, and being previously in the House of Lords about eight or nine hours; and having had to stand nearly all the time, I thought I would retire to bed and get about an hour's rest. But I could not sleep. In about an hour I got up and dipped a towel in cold water and gave my body a good rub all over and gave myself a good washing. After which, the whole day, I felt as if I had had a good night's rest. My friends remarked several times in the course of the day, "You look as fresh as if you had been in bed all night." It was the good washing which I had given myself that set me all right. I told them, what I very often tell when an opportunity offers itself, viz: when at home I have two good strong linen sheets, each about two yards and a half square; one I have wrung out of cold water, just dripping wet, and taken into my bedroom in a bucket. The first thing in the morning, when I get out of bed, I strip all off and take this dripping sheet out of the bucket, open it, and just put it over my back and head. First I give my back a good rubbing, and then all over my body, legs and feet; then I take the dry sheet which I have ready spread out on a chair back, which I put over my head, first rubbing my back and all over my body, legs and feet as before. Then I dress part way, shave and wash and dress out. In the course of my dressing I drink a glass or two of cold water, not drinking too much at a time, after which I am as cheerful as a lark in a fine summer's morning, and ready for a good walk or a good breakfast. This I have done every morning, when at home, for about 12 months, both winter and summer; and I find the colder the weather, and the more pleasant it is. It has taken all my rheumatism away and I need no doctor nor do I take any physic except physical exercise. If ever I am costive [constipated] I drink a glass or two more cold water in the morning before breakfast which generally sets me all right again. My regular plan is first thing after breakfast to go and get a stool, and for nearly thirty years I have punctually attended to this rule, with very few exceptions which has happened some few times when breakfasting with some friend and having got into some very interesting conversation and walking off with my friend, neglected the above rule, and forgot myself the whole day in consequence of which it has taken me near a fortnight before I would get myself quite right again. With the above treatment a person will seldom, if ever, have a bowel complaint or cholera.

About twenty-five or thirty years ago I was very subject to have the cholera; and about that time I had a most severe attack of that complaint. I sent for the doctor and told my wife to make me a treacle posset. She made a large jug full, of which I drank abundantly; it caused me to vomit very freely. When the doctor came, he said, "What have you been taking?" I told him a treacle posset. "What made you think of that?" I said, "I cannot tell." "Well," he said, "If you had not done so this complaint might have cost you your life, for it is a most severe attack of the cholera."

I mentioned this circumstance to a gentleman who usually dined with me in Manchester. He said, "I will tell you a secret related to me by a friend of mine who said: an old friend, a physician having given up business, I asked him to tell me a secret, viz: what is the best cure in case of cholera? The physician said, "Oh, wash out the kitchen, viz., drink warm water till you vomit freely two or three times and you will be all right." I thought, the first time I have another attack of the cholera I will try it, since which I have often tried it upon myself and family, and many others to whom I have mentioned it have tried it. I never knew or heard of a case if tried at the commencement of an attack of cholera where it did not effect a cure.

For a severe cholera or bowel complaint, take warm water till you vomit freely; repeat this three times then go to bed. You may take as much turkey rhubarb as you can put upon a sixpence, and most likely you will be well in the morning. Keep from butter or fat for a day or two, and you will be all right. I have tried it with good effect in my family for a headache, and for chilliness, shivering or being feverish. But it is still better to be enveloped in a wet sheet forty minutes and then take the shallow bath 75 degrees, then go to bed; and in the morning, take another envelope forty minutes, and then the dripping sheet. If properly attended to, it will set the person all right.

By attending to these things, my family have good health, seldom need a doctor or the use of physic. I have always found it a pleasure to me to tell these methods or rules to any who felt an interest in hearing them and not a few have told me since that they have adopted the above rules, and, whether in whole or in part, have thereby found very great benefit. We should always be trying to do some good both to the bodies and souls of our fellow men.

And I what a blessing has now been achieved for the labouring class in the repeal of the Corn Law, which Bill passed the third reading in the House of Lords June 25th 1846; to which the following day Her Majesty gave her Royal Assent. Soon after, at a meeting of the League, it was agreed that a sum of money should be raised as a national tribute to be given to Richard Cobden, Esq. who had devoted himself so much to the cause of Free Trade. My brothers and I put our names down for two hundred pounds, and in March 9th, 1847, we paid to the National Tribute for Richard Cobden, Esq. M.P., the sum of two hundred pounds. (say £200)

CORRESPONDENCE ON EDUCATION

But though this great question was now settled, I found there were other questions which philanthropy laid hold of my mind and forced me forward to action. The centralising illiberal measure proposed in the minutes of Council on Education, carries with it in my opinion a baneful influence upon all the rising generation; and if ever it is made to bear upon the people, it will enfeeble them almost to pauperisation.

The *Letters* to Lord John Russell by Edwd. Baines Esqr of Leeds are unanswerable. I wrote to Mr. Baines and told him if he published the "letters" we would take 100 copies for distribution. In a letter from him he stated to me, "When I was at the meeting of the Evangelical Alliance in Manchester, the Rev Dr Bunting, the Rev John Scott, Mr. Jas Wood and several others expressed their warm approbation of the *Letters*, and their hope that they would be published in another form." Mr. Baines published the *Letters* and we took 100 copies from him. I felt a desire that a number of them should be distributed to a number of our Wesleyan Preachers and I wrote to Dr Bunting to ask him to use his influence to get the Wesleyan Book room to send them in the Preachers book parcel, from whom I got the following answer.

(copy) London Decr. 24 1846

My Dear Friend,

I embraced the first opportunity of a meeting of the Book committee, after I received your letter, to mention to them your kind proposal respecting the distribution of Mr. Baines's valuable *Letters on Education*. We all felt obliged to you for your liberality. I were desirous, if we could with perfect propriety to have met your wishes. But we found that the established regulations respecting the conveyance of other Books than our own in our Monthly Parcels did not allow of such accommodation, and that an infringement of them would expose our Book Steward to *serious* inconvenience. Allow me to suggest that as Mr. Baines's own London Publishers (Simpkin & Marshall) send, I believe, weekly parcels to all part of the country, they might easily, be directed to forward a copy, suitably addressed, to the parties whom you wished to reach, if a list of those parties were forwarded first to them, with such request from you.

The subject is of immense importance so I hope will be well studied. May gracious Providence direct.

With sincere respect, I remain
Dear Friend
Yours truly
Jabez Bunting

From the above letter and the strange expressions used by Dr Bunting in the "Wesleyan Education committee" in London against the measure the minutes of council on Education. viz. that it was bad, irremediably bad &c, is evident proof of Dr Bunting's *Private opinion*. Soon after the "Education Committee" met in Manchester, when Mr. Heald of Stockport and a few more such gentlemen met with them some of whom had had an interview with Lord Ashley; after this meeting – did we hear any thing more said by Dr Bunting – only he said, it perhaps might be better to leave it an open question; what, better for Methodism if irremediably bad, or for Dr Bunting himself; was Dr Bunting really a free man in that meeting?

If riches amongst us can purchase a name.
The plague; it is enter'd and spreading again.

I saw at once the "Education Committee" was leaving all the Wesleyan Methodists in the dark upon the subject. But we thought we would do our duty at Rawtenstall, so we got up four Petitions to the House of Lords, one from the Wesleyan congregation, one from the Wesleyan School, one from Holly Mount School, and one from Rawtenstall and its vicinity. I addressed the following letter to Lord Morpeth: (copy)

Holly Mount, Rawtenstall, near Manchester.
My Lord,
I have for many years been a warm advocate for you on account of your liberal principles and I hope you will vote against that most

illiberal measure the minutes of council on Education, for from History and my own experience I am thoroughly convinced that any assistance by the state to the people only tends to Educate them to rely upon the state for everything, and thereby very much weaken their energies to help themselves, eventually may become feeble and helpless as the Irish people are at this present time; to make the nation healthy and strong the people must be taught to help themselves.

I hope you will also vote against the Factory Bill on the third reading, for this Bill if carried and persisted in, must be ruinous to the manufacturers of this country unless such a Measure could be obtained for the manufacturers of Foreign countries, and then it would be an unjust Law, because it would be injurious to the interest of the land, for we have ample proof of the *Truth* of Dr. A. Smith who says, in the conclusion of his last chapter in his first volume [of *The Wealth of Nations*, 1776], viz. "Every increase in the real wealth of the society, every increase in the quantity of useful labour employed within it, tends indirectly to raise the real rent of Land, a certain proportion of this labour naturally goes to the Land, a greater number of men and cattle are employed in its cultivation, the produce increases with the increase of the stock which is thus employed in raising it, and the rent increases with the produce. The contrary circumstances, the neglect of cultivation and improvement, the fall in the real price of any part of the rude produce of land, the rise in the real price of manufacturers from the *decay* of manufacturing art or *industry,* the declension of the real wealth of the society, all tend, on the other hand, to lower the real rent of land, to reduce *the real wealth of the Land lord*, to diminish his power of Purchasing either the labour or produce of the labours of other people."

As many of my friends in this neighbourhood who as well as myself have a vote for the West Riding of Yorkshire are of the same opinion and cannot in any way support the above measures.

              I have the Honor to be
                  My Lord
                      Your Lordships most obedient St.
                      David Whitehead

To the Right Honorable
Viscount Morpeth
April 15th 1847.

In my opinion State Education is the worst kind of centralization and the Wesleyan Education Committee have kept by far the greatest part of the Wesleyan Connection in the dark, and have thereby prevented their objecting to the "illiberal measures" proposed in the Minutes of Council on Education. The Factory Bill in principle is bad, it is bad in principle to legislate or enter into any combination for any class of labourers whether they be labourers to produce clothing, or food, or Buildings for the use of man and cattle; or roads, railways, and canals, for the use of conveyance for the good of the human family; man only requires for the body while in this world, food and clothing, and buildings to screen him from the inclemency of the weather; and all the different classes of labourers in producing these necessaries of life should have fair play. To give protection to one class of labourers, will injure somewhere another class of labourers; for instance, if you by an Act of Parliament lessen the labour of producers of clothing Factories, it must either reduce the wages of the producers of cloth or increase the value of the cloth, in either case it will injure some other class of producers, for if their wages are less they cannot use so much of the productions of some other class of labourers, who would be injured thereby, and if the cloth be increased in value the other classes of labourers would have to pay the difference or do without their productions, which would be hard upon the poor needlewomen of London of whom so much have been said about them working, 16, and 18 hours per day for which each would receive from fourpence to six pence, and then, through class legislation would have to pay more for their clothing, in this way grinding the poorest of the poor by class legislation, in fact class legislation always run to this point, to oppress the poorest of the poor. It will be a great blessing for the world when Governments are made to do their own business, protect life and property, and "let alone" the people to do their own business themselves. A-many hard things have been said of the employers of poor labourers for want of more light upon the subject; employers do not in any case eventually lower wages, it is always the employed, who are too many upon the market and bid one against another and in this way reduce wages, which is a proof there are too many labourers for that kind of labour; if two labourers of equal abilities come to an employer and one will work for less wages than the other, the employer to be just must employ the labourer who will do it for the least because most needy, on the contrary if two employers equal in every other respect are offering higher wages to obtain labourers, the labourer inquiring for work to be just must work for the employer who bids the highest price, so employers advance wages, and labourers reduce wages, according to circumstances. When there are too many labourers at one kind of work, they should be instructed to find some other kind of employment, if all were determined to make hats we should die for want of food; if there are too many needle women in London instead of societies being got up who rake up all their malice upon the employers of the needle women, saying all kinds of hard things against those who are their best friends; societies should be got up to instruct the poor ignorant people to get some other employment either in their own neighbourhood or in some other country, and thereby equalise labour, it cannot be done by legislation, but a great deal may be done by human societies, in distributing tracts upon the subject amongst the labouring people, and in other ways, lecturing and teaching the poor ignorant labourers common sense. The temperance societies has done more good the last twenty years to the people in getting them to abstain from intoxicating drink than all the Acts of Parliament ever made for that purpose. Query: Has not the tax laid upon intoxicating drink made it more respectable and rather encouraged drinking than otherwise? It would be wise for the community to take a lesson from the temperance society and try to do good in the same way, where legislation cannot reach, and by which it should never be attempted. A Gentleman once said to me that in his opinion Moses of London[7] was one of the most tyrannical men in the world, giving such miserable low wages to the needle women and putting up his blazing advertisements enough to frighten a horse when passing by them. I said if Moses did not employ those poor women what must become of them? Whatever may be the motive of Moses for employing them, it is better that they are employed by him than if they had no employment at all, it appears that he is their best friend; and we have no right to call in question his motive; he might do what he is doing from the best of motives, he might see all these poor women upon the market for employment, and say to himself, I will employ my capital in finding these poor women some employment, and that I may be enabled to find more employment for a greater number of them I will put up blazing advertisements and I will sell as low as I can that I may do more business and give more employment. Moses cannot lay hold of these poor women and say come I will make you work for me at my price, but he will be obliged to give such wages at which he can get them to work, and if there be too many needlewomen upon the market it is not Moses' fault, so we should let the blame fall in its proper place; if the evil were fully understood and taken up by the community it would be more than half the cure. Some people seem to think that every evil should be cured by legislation, which in many cases cannot be done without creating a greater evil, by relieving the imprudent and throwing the evil upon the prudent, this kind of legislation should never be attempted; for instance, the distressing times of 1847 which was brought on in part by the monomania of railway making, not that railways are an evil, but a real good; but the country went mad upon railway making all at once and took the labourers from making food to making railways, it never entered into the mind of some people that railways are made with Beef, Bacon, Corn bread etc., just think; the labourers eat the food while they are making the railways, but the railways produce no food, railways are fixt capital; and any country which fix more capital than its profits, must suffer in proportion; then, when food became scarce, speculation sprung up, and at this time some have gone mad in that, and are involved to such an extent that they had to go for help to the Bank of England; in consequence of the high price of corn, the Gold had left the Bank, and the help to the extent they wanted could not be had there: then they wanted the Government to legislate and issue one pound notes and thus mortgage the nation to procure more money in order to hold their corn for higher prices, and so punish the poor so much the more. They also employed the printing press upon the subject, some of whom my Brothers and I had formed a very high opinion were not going wrong, so in accordance with my Brothers I wrote the following "privet letter" to the Editor of the "Economist", London:(copy).

Holly Mount,
Rawtenstall
May 12th 1847

Dear Sir

From the commencement of the "Economist" we have thought it the soundest commercial paper ever published in the world, and have felt proud that England had such a publication, until the article on the "present crisis, its character and remedy," appeared in the Economist of May 8th which appeared to us to be far from good sound Policy as regards the alteration of the currency. [This is] because to issue one pound notes will be very injurious both to the manufacturers and agriculture; wages now paid for making railways are such as neither manufacturers nor agriculturists can afford to pay; they are unnaturally high, because railway making is now forced beyond what the country can afford, therefore the labour is drawn from its legitimate source, and thereby lessening our production of food; and to make money more easy, by issuing one pound notes would very much increase this evil: then again, as food advances the community are less able to buy clothing, and cotton advancing still adds to the distress of manufacturers and labourers of all except those employed by the monomania of railway making. Corn and cotton, their stocks being low would advance very much, but it would be contrary with manufacturers, their stocks are very large, and although so much short time is being worked, they are accumulating, and declining in price, and to issue one pound notes would be class legislating against the prudent part of the community of a most unjust kind. The wisest plan that can be adopted by Government at the present time is just to do nothing; if the present dispute is left to take its natural course; discounts will run high, which is the only legitimate way to set imprudent men right. We wish to know when you increase the Government securities from £14,000,000 to £34,000,000 are you not making £20,000,000 of fixt capital into floating capital? And we must confess we cannot understand in what way you have Sir Robert Peel with you in the proposed alteration of the currency; either we do not understand you or we never properly understood Sir Robert Peel. Would he go to increase Government securities and thereby take still more fixed capital and make it into floating capital; we have understood him just to the contrary, and we have you with him in opinion upon the currency ever since he came out upon the subject (say 1818) and up to the present time we have thought him the wisest and soundest public man in the world upon the currency question. Should it turn out that we have not understood him and that he is with you on your proposed alteration, we must acknowledge we have not seen any thing to change our opinion and we shall have much to learn or unlearn before we can alter our present views.

We are dear Sir
Yours very respectfully
Tho. Whitehead & Brothers

To the Editor of the Economist, London

Holly Mount, Rawtenstall,
19 May 1847

Dear Sir

Please pardon our intrusion on your time for a few minutes, we should not have written to you at all but for the high opinion we have had of the "Economist." The article on the currency of the 15th Inst. is only going on in the wrong direction (excuse our honesty). The proposed plan is artificial to meet the present crisis and so calculated as to relieve the imprudent and throw the burden upon the prudent commercial and labouring men. You say it would not increase the price of Corn and Cotton, how is it then that the slightest ease in money and up goes cotton, it would undoubtedly advance the price of both Corn and Cotton; holders would be able to hold for in advance and would get it too, and if Gold was sent out for Corn and Cotton, would it not advance in Foreign Markets, then if Corn and Cotton declined in price in consequence of great importations must it not be ruinous to they importers; the plan will not work well. Would not the present holders of Corn and Cotton just like to shove off their stocks at the advance upon the Manufacturers, shop keepers and the labouring people, leaving them to deal with the plan as they could: the holders have a right to get their stocks off for the best price they can, but to adapt an artificial plan to enable them to get their stocks off at high prices is unjust. The distress we are labouring under at present is not for want of money, it is mainly because of short supply of food partly caused by railway speculation, and if holders want money let them go to manufacturers, shop keepers, and labourers, and not to an artificial plan, you may depend upon it we are not short of money in the country if holders will only take the price people are willing to give, if holders of Cotton want money let them come to us manufacturers we will find them money if they will take our price: then let us have fair play and no class legislation; the nearer we can come and keep to a metallic currency and the better for all classes, we are not in the habit of writing or we should have entered more into the subject, nor should we have written to you but we feel so sorry that such a sudden change had taken place. The currency has not been a thing of today with us, and we are certain the nearer any nation (or even firm) can come to a metallic currency and the better it will be for them both as regards wealth and morals, which in fact is coming nearer to a ready money system, we know some say we could not do as much business upon the ready money system, which is a very great fallacy, we think we have proof of this by experience. This is a subject of great importance to any people and would require much to be said to make it perfectly clear.

>We are Dear Sir yours
>very respectfully
>Thos. Whitehead & Brothers

To the Editor of The Economist, London

P.S. The question upon state Education is not yet settled, we have been well pleased with what you have said upon that subject, less the state meddles with us and better.

According to the plan proposed in the "Economist", the 20,000,000 of Gold which would be added to the effective capital of the country would be a mortgage upon fixed capital of the country, the interest of which must be paid by somebody. Mortgaging fixed capital in order to fix more capital is, along with the delay of the repeal of the "Corn Laws" the primary cause of the present distress, this country has been fixing much more capital in railways, Mills and Machinery, than its profits, and to do this it has been obliged to mortgage, and the high rates paid for money and wages has drawn both capital and labour from the producers of food, and nothing can bring us right but speculators of this kind being brought to their right mind; so that a proper proportion of capital and labour may flow into the production of corn and other produce. Manufacturers may mortgage their mills to increase their floating capital, but to mortgage in order to fix more capital is not a sound plan to pursue because the interest of the mortgage must be paid whether they can work their mill to profit or not, if they have no mortgage they can work their mills at one, two, or three per cent, sooner than let them stand [i.e. be unemployed] and so compete with foreign manufacturers; no doubt but many concerns have gone on in mortgaging fixt capital and fixing more capital until they have by this unsound plan, after consuming a large capital taken into the concern become bankrupts. The safest plan for a concern whether it be small or large, is to have for the business it is doing a proper amount of floating capital and the rest of its capital maybe fixed capital and it may continue to fix more capital, according to its profits always taking care to reserve a proper amount of floating capital to carry on its business; all concerns that pay strict attention to this plan and are delinquent in their business may reasonably expect to prosper and will have no fear of ever becoming bankrupts; if a concern deviate from this most sound plan, then it becomes a matter of opinion how far they may prudently go from it, if a person entering into business has no capital but fixt capital it would be better to mortgage part of the fixt capital to procure a floating capital than to do his business all on credit, but for any concern or nation to mortgage fixt capital in order to fix more capital is dangerous to such concerns or Nation and to pursue it is inevitable ruin.

Take an illustration. A, who has a capital of £60,000, £50,000 of which he lays out in a Mill and Machinery for the Manufacture of cotton, the remaining £10,000 he has for floating capital to carry on his business, after getting this mill to work and anxious to extend his business he mortgages this mill and builds another and goes onto mortgage again and build again, until he finds that he is short of floating capital to carry on his business. After this, A meets with B, who has a large capital at command which he wants to employ, but whether A asks B for assistance or B offer to lend A assistance I cannot tell. But one night when in Liverpool on inquiring in an Inn for a bed I was introduced to a Gentleman of a House who were said to be wealthy, this Gentleman knew me very well, and they were that night short of single bed rooms in the Inn, he said to the Landlady, he should be glad to have Mr. Whitehead as a companion with him in a double bedded room, which was agreed upon. When we got up in the morning and while dressing ourselves this Gentleman became very friendly in conversation and said "Mr. Whitehead we have been taking notice of your firm for some time and have confidence in you, and if at anytime you want to speculate in cotton you may draw bills upon us and we will accept them providing you buy your cotton through our broker and allow us one eighth per lb upon what you buy this way." I said "I am obliged to you for your offer but we are bound by our partnership agreement not to draw any Bills of accommodation," he said you can talk it over and if you alter your mind we will render you this assistance and at some times it may be of service; but Brothers and I have made up our minds that we would never avail ourselves of so dangerous an assistance. But to continue the illustration, A avails himself of the assistance to draw Bills upon B, and buy his cotton through B's broker and allow B one eighth per lb for the accommodation, after A has you on the way for some time and trade not so good B tells A that money is becoming scarcer and discounts higher and that they must now have more allowed them for their assistance but if B finds A not willing and fears A will try to get help from some other source, B says oh well never mind we will go on there perhaps may be a turn soon; then B will be more liberal and encourage A to do more business, and when B finds he has got A in his books so far that he cannot loose himself, B says to A the account is so large we must have some security, and compels A to show his whole concern's affair and make over all the property which is not already mortgaged to B, then B gets to know what the concern will make, and takes good care to charge A as much for his accommodation as the concern will make, and if trade be good and the concern will make a good profit B may keep A in this way for years, say until there is a succession of failing crops which always brings more or less of bad trade and distress in the country, then B begins to speak well of A, setting him up for a great man of business and saying many other great thing about him and at the same time advising A to get credit elsewhere and in this way B gets A to reduce his account with him as far as he possibly can, and when B finds that A cannot reduce his account any more, and trade being now so bad, and A is loosing by his concern; in fact when B finds he has got all the capital which A possessed and all the profit he could get out of his concern, and involved him in debt as much as possible elsewhere to reduce B's account with A, then B makes A bankrupt and becomes himself a heavy creditor to share the spoil, after having drained off all he could from A and all he could get A to drain from others, thus by pursuing artificial instead of sound plans A looses a capital of £60,000 after many years of anxiety and trouble, and in the end as regard this world becomes a ruined man. "They that will be such fall into temptation and a snare" and "wealth gotten by vanity shall be diminished: but he that gathereth by labour shall increase," so, for any concern or Nation to mortgage fixt capital in order to fix more capital is dangerous to such a concern or nation. This nation has already upon it far too heavy a Mortgage, and the people of the Nation have to pay the interest, a burden heavy enough without increasing it by issuing one pound notes and thereby making £20,000,000 of fixt capital into floating capital which would increase the government securities £20,000,000 the interest of which would have to be paid by the people. The nearer we can keep to a Metallic currency and the better for the community. The grand secret is just here; it is better to do our business with ready money than upon credit; so he that would do better and be happy and enjoy business all his life, must never attempt to do more business than he has capital at his own command.

THE 1848 CRISIS

Though short crops of corn, partly brought on by railway speculation and building new mills, fixing more capital in the country than its profits, thereby drawing labour from the production of food and the potato rot, together with the Corn Laws, made food scarce and dear, so that the people could not buy much clothing. A many could scarcely get sufficient of food. In consequence of which, in the Spring of 1848 trade became very bad and much distress in the manufacturing districts, and those who had not made much improvements in their machinery began to lower wages, against which the workpeople turned out. We had made great improvements in our power looms, through which each weaver could tend three looms as well as they could before tend two. The improvement had cost us more than a thousand pounds, which enabled each three-loom weaver, at two pence per piece less for weaving, to get above one shilling per week more upon the improved looms. It is now near six years since we made the improvements. These improvements had not been made at Bacup, but the manufacturers lowered their wages though they had not made the improvement. The weavers in that neighbourhood,

I believe through ignorance, had strong objections to weave on three looms upon the improved plan; they all turned out and after they had been out for some time, began to come in procession past our Mill, when our Mill was loosing for dinner and shouted the workpeople to get them to turn out and intermixed with them, and as many as would hearken to them, they tried to persuade to turn out. We had never had any complaints about wages from our weavers nor had we altered our wages for near six years, and had no idea that the turnouts would make any impression upon them. But they did eventually persuade a part of them, and about one half of our weavers in our Lower Rawtenstall Mill turned out.

I informed them that they must return to their work, and if they wished to leave they must give us regular notice. But they paid no attention, so we took out summons for a few of them to appear before the Magistrates.

In the meantime, they used every plan they could invent to get the remainder to turn out; they walked with them from the Mill to their houses at the mealtimes, and back again to the Mill, but with all their artful intimidation and persuasion could not succeed. A many of those workpeople who remained at their work had been in our employ a long time, a goodly number from twenty to thirty years, and not a few of them like ourselves, were against combination of Class against Class, and all class legislation. Combination of class against class is just as bad as class legislation so long as they stand true to their scheme. All combinations are bad except to disseminate true principles. Combination of class against class is not a true principle and will not work well for the community. If work people may combine and stipulate what wages their employers shall give, then their employers may combine and stipulate what wages they will pay and how much per lb they will give for cotton and also what price they would have for their manufactured goods; and then buyers of goods may combine and stipulate what they would give for goods, and cotton merchants and so on to cotton planters may combine and say what price they would have for their cotton and likewise all other trades. In this way there would be a continual war in the commercial world with each other of these great combinations of class against class. Business could not be carried on this way, therefore the principle is not true and should not be tolerated. The true principle is for employers to buy the raw material and labour in the cheapest market and sell their manufactured goods in the dearest, and the labourer to buy his food and clothing in the cheapest market and sell his labour in the dearest, and all contracts and agreements both with employers and labourers to be duly reformed.

About twenty years ago, there was a turnout of [calico] printers at Crawshawbooth. The contest was a most severe one and lasted a long time. Eventually the principal had to get the soldiers to guard the works and the workpeople for a considerable length of time. Seeing the evil of combinations and turnouts, and particularly the above turnout, brothers and I at that time agreed that, if ever our workpeople turned out in a body, that we would not have anything to say to them as a body. As we contracted with them singly or by families, we would hear them each for themselves as we had engaged them, and no other way; and that if the people, or a part of them, combined to leave our employ all at once that we would not employ them again upon any terms whatever. We came to this conclusion in order to put a stop to any contest betwixt us and the workpeople, so that they might at once get employment elsewhere, and we would begin again and engage workpeople in the usual way. Now the time had arrived when our plan had to be tested.

The workmen whom we had summoned appeared at the appointed time before the Magistrates, who decided they should give us a month's notice before they left our employ; which was according to our regular agreement when we engaged them – to give or take a month's notice. My brother Peter being from home at the time, the management of the affair fell on me. The morning after the decision of the Magistrates, it being Tuesday and having to go to Manchester, I had only time to give notice to a few of those whom I knew to have been the leading men in this turnout. I left orders that the rest might go to their work, and from all who wished to give notice I would take it the next day, as I could only take their notice separately in the way we had engaged them and would have to see them personally, and enter the names of all those who might give notice in a book, that there might be no misunderstanding afterwards. A many of them came to me and said that they would not go to their work till they had given notice. I told them that they might go to their work, for, as many as gave notice, I would take notice from that day, but as I had to go to Manchester, I could not attend to it then. So they might go to their work, as it would make no difference whatever. But they would only go to their work as they gave notice. On Wednesday I began to take their notices, and as they came to give notice, I told them that an agreement had been made some time ago betwixt us as partners, that if our workpeople all or part of them, should turn out and give us notice all at a time that we would not employ them again upon any terms. I distinctly told them that if they gave me notice, I must enter their names in that book (a book prepared for that purpose), and if their names were found in that book, they could not be employed by us any more after their notice had run out. I invariably inquired of each as they came before me, what they had turned out for, and with what they were dissatisfied. Some said they could not tell, some said they were satisfied and did not want to turn out. Some said because the turn-outs shouted us so, some because they did not like to be shouted at. I said, "No more do I, but if that was all, you should have kept on my side and helped me to shout." Some said that the turn-outs said it was "because we would not turn out that they were out, and we did not like it." But there was not one, in all who gave me notice, would say they wanted more wages. I told them that it was very strange, for them to give me notice without any complaints but such as those numerated above, and that I was very sorry they were giving me notice; they would very soon be as sorry as me, and would come and beg and cry, and beg of us to take them in again, when it would be entirely out of our power, for we could not break our agreement.

This being the case, I took two days in taking their notices. I spent a great deal of time in explaining to them, that, if they gave notice, we would not on any account take them on again; and that, if they had not thought it over, they might go to their work and take a week or two to think about it, and if they after that remained in the same mind, and came and gave me notice, I would take it as though they had given it me this day. Because, I told them, I was sure, if their names got into that book, they could not be employed with us again, except some name should get into the book through some one giving notice who could afterwards be proved not to have had authority to give such notice.

Some took the advice and took time to consider; others, after all I could say, were determined to give notice, and some told me after all I had said, that we should take them on again. Some did not give notice, but, through fear, told others that they had done so; some, who had taken time to consider, through persuasion or fear, came again and gave notice. I advised all who did give notice to be sure to look out for another shop, for I was sure they could not have any more work with us. I further told them that if any of them wanted a character, I would give them one as I had nothing against them, and as they had turned out and through which they had given us notice, in consequence of which I knew we could not employ them again, I felt wishful to do all I could to get them into work elsewhere.

But the hardest thing had yet to come. As the end of their notice drew near they came to me, one after another, begging and crying, and wishing me to take them on again. I told them I could not do anything of the kind, and reminded them that I distinctly told them that if they gave me notice we could not employ them again, and now it was out of my power. They said they repented for what they had done, and thought we should forgive them. I said we did forgive you for turning out, in that you did us wrong. But we gave you liberty to go to your work again without notice, but you had a legal right to give us notice in that you have done us no wrong. Therefore we have nothing against you, but we cannot break our agreement, which prevents us for employing you again. All those who had given us notice at the expiration of such notice were obliged to leave our employ. Consequently, there were no contest between the workpeople and us.

At the commencement of this turn-out, about a month ago, a many bad things were said against us in the country, and now the country says they were false reports, and we were right, and the turn-outs [strikers] have made a great mistake. Fresh hands applied for work, and the vacant places filled up sooner than we could reasonably have expected. I did nothing in this without much prayer and I believe I was divinely assisted.

We had two hundred new [power] looms and spinning machinery for the same which had not yet commenced working. The unfavourable reports which got out into the country through the turn-out when the reaction took place which was very soon, we have reason to believe worked for our good, for hands continued to apply [for employment at the mill] as fast as we could get the machinery ready for them, till completed. Brothers and I made our mind up not to enlarge our works for the present.

Having been about fifteen years constantly building, or putting new machinery to work, in the course of which time we have built Holly Mount, and Holly Mount School, also eighty cottage houses, and mills and sheds, in which we have upwards of one thousand power looms, and machinery to spin twist and weft for the same; we have had much labour of body and mind in all this work, and much pleasure, and abundant cause of thankfulness to God for the preservation of the lives of ourselves, and all our workmen in the execution of all this work, and work too, of which there is often so much danger. Praise the Lord the earth is the Lord's, for He has redeemed us with his blood, and may we and all our families constantly enjoy the adoption into His family and avail ourselves of our glorious privilege to serve the Lord in all our work and in all we do, whether we eat or drink, or whatsoever we do may we do [it] with a single eye to the glory of God. Amen.

[The autobiography continues with a long passage (pp. 206-225) describing the visit of Whitehead and his family to the Paris Peace Congress in August 1849. "I believe the Peace Society is of God and I feel myself highly honoured by Him that He will allow me to be one of the instruments in His hand to bring about his own design ... war shall come to an end for thus saith the prophet Isaiah." Whitehead revealed himself to be an enthusiastic follower of Richard Cobden, one of the Congress's leaders, but otherwise disclosed nothing of his political ideology in this passage, his text being essentially a tourist's commentary without significant interpretation of his understanding of it. His concluding thought was to compare the over centralising administration of the Wesleyan Church with those of Metternich and Louis Philippe (pp.225-9), more particularly in education, as he had expressed forcibly in a long letter to the *Wesleyan Times*, 3 Dec 1849.]

THE PEACE SOCIETY

This year [1849] at Rawtenstall we established a branch of the Peace Society. Brother Peter and I were appointed delegates to go to the Peace Congress to be held at Brussels in September. Brother Peter and I went as delegates, my wife and brother's wife and his daughter Marianne as friends. We all left Holly Mount on Monday, the 18th September for London, and met the delegates the same evening at six o'clock at the Hall of Commerce, Threadneedle Street, London. At nine o'clock we proceeded from the Hall of Commerce by railway to Blackwall. Tea was provided for the party at the Brunswick Hotel, Blackwall, after which we embarked aboard the steamship. But being a dense fog, we had to stop in the river all night. It was intended for us to arrive at Ostend about three o'clock on Friday afternoon.

[The following pages are largely devoted to an uncritical tourist's account of Brussels and some summaries of the congress session meetings. There is nothing of personal interest to Whitehead].

This day, August 29th I arrived [back] at Holly Mount. Home sweet home, there is no place like home. Praise the Lord for home. I would ever acknowledge God for his goodness in all things, and I pray that may be made instrumental in his hands of doing the world good, in civilisation and commercially, politically and religiously. I always feel a desire to leave the world better than when I came into it. I have no doubt but the Friends of Peace have left a good impression in France and have been made a great blessing to them. Some seed have been sown which will bring forth some fruit that will be seen many days hence. The French people if once set right in religion will be a fine people; they are not a drinking people, they have good taste; they want setting right in religion. May God in his mercy speedily bring it about, for Christ's sake Amen.

THE WESLEYAN 'FLY SHEET' CONTROVERSY

My wife and daughter, Sarah, left Paris on Thursday August 30th and arrived in London on Friday August 31st, that memorable day on which that great meeting took place in Exeter Hall to hear the statements of the expelled Wesleyan ministers, the Reverend Messrs. Everett,[8] Dunn,[9] and Griffith.[10] My wife and daughter both attended that meeting and had the happiness of being introduced to and shaking hands once more with that great and good man, Mr. Everett. Being in goodtime they got a good situation in the hall. Accidentally very near to Mrs. Beaumont. As soon as my wife saw her though she had never seen her before, it was impressed upon her mind that that lady was Doctor Beaumont's wife. She enquired and found that the impression on her mind was correct.

She introduced herself to Mrs. Beaumont and made some enquiry about the Doctor, and gave her to understand that he was a great favourite in our family.

At half past six, the time when the meeting was announced to commence, the spacious hall presented one dense mass of living beings. The attention kept up by the speakers throughout the whole of the meeting, and the unanimous responses made to the sentiments they advanced, and the weight of pious and moral influence upon the platform, had not the minds of the leading men of conference been darkened through making themselves necessitated to rich men, they would at once have seen their great mistake. "Methodism as it is," without any doubt needs reforming, ample proof of which may be had from the conference party themselves. Are they not on every side expelling members; as they say bad members, viz: bad Methodists, "as it is."

What numbers of its fruits are bad; then how bad must be the tree. How many of its fruits have been cast away as being bad within the last thirty years, and what is the watchman, the organ of the conference party now saying about Methodist reformers? To what does he liken them unto? I need not mention here, but does he not make it out that they are very, very naughty – so very bad that they are not fit for Methodism as it is? Just see are they not the fruits of Methodism as it is? Then Methodism as it is cannot be a good tree: "For a good tree bringeth not forth corrupt fruit" and "every tree is known by his own fruit"– the fruit be bad the tree must be bad also, and Methodism as it is, out of the mouths of the conference party themselves, is condemned. And I have no doubt but God is speaking by the people. "The axe is laid into the root of the trees; therefore every tree which bringeth not forth good fruit is hewn down and cast into the fire".

I pray that the Wesleyan reformers, through the help of God, may be able to save Wesleyan Methodism from that most awful catastrophe, though all human systems as scaffolding will be burnt in the end. Yet may the Wesleyan Methodist scaffold be so reformed or made safe till the work be completed, that there may not be in the accomplishment of the work so many lives lost. It has long been my opinion that "Methodism as it is" is very bad, and without a great reform the Wesleyan Methodists cannot prosper as a church of Christ, But my views perhaps will be as fully stated as anything I can say in the following which was published in the *Wesleyan Times* of December 3rd, 1849.

> Dear Sirs, –
>
> A few days ago a person put into my hand "The Fly Sheets."[11] I had not read them before with the exception, I think of number one; and after looking them over I confess to have seen little more in them with regard to centralisation and secularisation than what had been known to myself, as well as dreaded by many other Wesleyan Methodists for some length of time. The work of centralisation has been going on in Methodism, I repeat it, for the last thirty years to my certain knowledge; and I have not hesitated on various occasions to point out the evil consequences of such a system to many with whom I have conversed on the subject. The recollection of which I have no doubt, will be vivid to such persons as may favour these remarks with a perusal. "The Fly Sheets" have, in principle at least, very little but what was known, felt and canvassed out of conference in different Wesleyan circles before. Why then this mighty stir? I know no reason why, unless it be that those who are placed at the head of affairs, and so aiding the centralization system, are like men who, living in the neighbourhood of a volcano and having no knowledge of what is going on around and beneath, are nevertheless afraid of some sudden alarm from the circumstance of a few sparks – say the "Fly Sheets" – instantly issuing from some unapprehended crevice.
>
> What was known by Metternich and Louis Philippe, both of whom were carrying centralization as they thought, to the highest forms of perfection respecting the views and movements of the masses of society beneath them? Comparatively nothing, till the whole blew up like one of the eruptions of Vesuvius or Etna, themselves barely escaping with their lives. Centralization may suit the purpose of tyrants, but a wise people will never allow it to go on. There are many who do not appear to know what is meant by centralization. Take an illustration: Centralization may be compared to water confined within a given space by embankments. But mark, if on collecting

a number of small streams together into one reservoir you are not careful to keep all safe then, like centralization, these concentrated streams will be in danger of inundating all below by carrying away the embankments. Should anyone, whether from good or bad motives, let off the water it would, however small the stream at first, draw off the whole and prove destructive to all within its influence.

The object of centralization both in church and state is to bind the collective streams together to legislate so as to bind the people to certain restrictive laws which prevents the free expression of opinion; the person thus binding and concentrating, checking, altering, and directing the course of the people agreeably to his will. None but God, who has set bounds to the sea, should have this power, and even this power he does not in the fullest sense exert, in as much as he leaves man a free agent. The power claimed by centralizing man is a power too great for him to wield, and therefore ought never to be ceded. It is equally dangerous to subject and ruler. The man who grasps after it is but a boy when placed by the side of a man of common sense.

Children – I have done it myself – are in the habit of binding the water as it flows down the channels after a shower of rain: but they as often find their little embankments carried away. Look at Metternich – look at Louis Phillipe! What were they when binding the people by centralization? Their schemes like the letting off of water broke down their own embankments, and the people once set free swept all before them like a devastating flood.

Centralizers are but the older boys, and the more mischievous, who are stopping up the channels; they are unworthy [of] the name of men, if not the "bigger boys" of creation. When a good man works his way to the head of centralization the danger becomes greater. He reasons thus: "There is no power but of God. For the power which he hath given me I am responsible." What he therefore conceives to be right he feels bound in conscience to carry out. He at once lays hold of that human invention, centralization, too unwieldy an instrument for any man to use; but which having been constructed at great cost he resolves to employ against others, and is at length overwhelmed by it himself. The Divine Being can centralize to any extent – lay and can manage it too: not so ambitious selfish man.

Centralization is no novelty with me. Adverting some mss. notes made some time ago, I find a reference to the trouble which we had in the Bacup circuit to get up and to present a petition to the conference against the theological institution. I objected to it because it partook too much of the nature of the system of centralization. There was virtually a concentrated power over the conference; and besides it does not require a man of extensive learning to preach the Gospel. A man of good common sense, deep piety, and ardent zeal will find his way to the heads and hearts of the people with the readiness and success of a primitive apostle. John Wesley did right in sending the boys to school, but I have my doubts whether it is right to send a man to school whom God has called and fitted in his own way to preach the gospel.

God took Moses when a 'babe' and sent him to Pharaoh's daughter under whose care he received a first rate education – Egyptian, of course, in its character, but even that was sufficient under God. On Moses arriving at mature years, he was sent in the order of Divine Providence, to tend the flock of Jethro, and to acquire a little agricultural knowledge. After this he was called to be a leader and teacher of the people. When God was in want of a man of learning, he sent for Saul of Tarsus. I am no enemy to education. I have given full proof of that – only let it be of the right kind. Educate the child the youth – up to manhood if you please, but when God calls a man to preach the gospel do not mar him afterwards by sending him to school. He may learn Methodism, but will his preaching be as productive in the salvation of souls? If the Theological Institution is to be useful to Methodism, it must be differently constituted to what it is. A school should have no power over the Church of God, no more than the state itself. They are both of this world and Christ is the head of the Church. The Church can acknowledge neither school nor state as its head, whether to rule or to legislate. We in the Bacup circuit gave the free expression of our thoughts to Conference, kept firmly united, did that which we believed to be best for Methodism, and rejoiced in the fact that we had no divisions – not that I think divisions are always bad. We should perhaps not be so well satisfied, or even prosper so much if we had only one Wesleyan Conference in England. There are three Methodist conferences – that of the New Connection, the Primitive, and the Wesleyan Association. Had the old connection had no division, the conference might have been foolish enough to build a Babel of its own; and God may yet see it proper to confound the "Society" in its language for going astray, preventing the members from understanding one another, and so scattering them over the earth.

Since the period referred to my views and convictions have undergone no change with regard to centralization, nor any in reference to state education which is the worst kind of centralization. The latter is snare laid to entrap the people and is as subtle as the serpent in the garden of Eden. The Churches that are caught by it will have to smart for it. Why; it will pauperise them; they will be educated into the belief that they cannot help themselves. The people should be taught the fact — they should know it that they can educate themselves; that they have in themselves a richer mine, than is to be found in California — a mine in which they themselves should dig, and while they try, the God that made them will help them too. History and experience teach us that any assistance afforded by the state only tends to educate the people to rely upon that state. Rely upon the state for one thing, and you will rely upon it for another. In this way the energies of the people are weakened; they cease to help themselves, and eventually become as feeble and helpless as the Irish during the potato rot, or as the Communists of France in the rebellion of 1848 who had been taught, or in another word educated to look to the state for everything.

Such are my convictions of the evil of centralization that I have employed both money and personal influence to oppose it. The illiberal measures proposed in the minutes of the Council on Education, so argumentatively and statistically combatted by Edward Baines esq., of Leeds will not be soon forgotten. It is a source of deep regret to many and also to myself that the committees and Conference of the Wesleyan Methodists should have done more towards the support of the centralization system, not only in the body but in the state, than any other Christian community in the land making the least profession of the voluntary principle. Centralization in the state is pauperisation to the people; and carried into the church it is the bane of all true religion. The people must voluntarily educate themselves. This will relieve them of their shackles; and this must be done, before wars shall come to an end — before truth peace and righteousness can be established in the earth. The time will come, God has said it, and it shall come to pass (may he hasten the time), and may the people pray, believe, and work, and so help forward the 'ark of God.'

> David Whitehead
> Holly mount, Rawtenstall
> November 26th, 1849

There is no doubt in my mind but the movement which is now agitating the Wesleyan Methodist Church is of God, who in his providence is bringing about either a great division or a great reform in that Church. I think the latter is the most probable. A division will not leave her in a prosperous and sound state. A great number of her members are of families yet alive, to the third and fourth generation. If a division takes place, what a rend in such families! Those of them who would not leave will be dissatisfied, and their children intermingling with those of their relations who leave the connection would hear their objections by "Methodism as it is."

After such a division there might be a lull and the calm for a time, succeeded by a reaction, and then the thousands and tens of thousands of families who will be gathered around their fires in the long winter nights, murmuring over the separation of their relations and choice friends, they will then begin to see things as they did not see them before, and the hundreds of preachers and their wives and children who will not be altogether free from the same thing. While these murmurings are going on like a hidden fire in some large manufacture, the managers of which, not being aware of anything of the kind, sleeping contentedly in bed till alarmed by the dreadful catastrophe so while the few who are managing Methodism (all in London) are sleeping in their supposed security, these fireside family murmurings will be going on like hidden fire, getting faster and faster hold and producing a greater than ever dissatisfaction to "Methodism as it is." Which, with its present centralization, would not take more than ten or fifteen years before there would be another eruption. Therefore I think the providential way is not to leave the church, whatsoever persecution may have to be endured. I am aware the local preachers are peculiarly situated, being called of God to preach his word, and dare not give it up, and the conference can, if it see fit, stop any preacher from preaching in any of its chapels. But the preachers have the plan of our venerable founder of Methodism, John Wesley to fall back upon. When the churches were shut against John Wesley, he preached out of doors and in barns or where he could. God owned his labours; people were converted. Observe, he did not preach in the church hours, but advised the people to go to church. Let the preachers, against who the pulpits are closed do likewise, not preaching in chapel hours, but at other times, and advise the people to attend the chapel and not to leave the church. Had the Church of England in John Wesley's time been a voluntary church, query, would not John Wesley and his coadjutors have reformed the whole Protestant Church of England. The Wesleyan Methodist Church is a voluntary church, and a real John Wesleyan in the fullest sense will make the best reformer of "Methodism as it is." Read his works, let his political and scriptural plan of evangelising the world be adopted. He laboured for the conversion of souls, but said do not leave the church. Then let all reformers pray in faith, and labour on in love to Christ, for a perishing world, and keep to the church which they have so long laboured and for which they have so often prayed. Watch the opining of providence and walk in the light of his countenance and God will make the reform which he intends to bring about to appear clear, and what he purposes to do, no other power can frustrate. These being my views I have not failed, nor shall I fail, to give my opinion and advise accordingly both to Wesleyan reformers and Wesleyan preachers, and to those who may be, or may appear to be, on the Conference side, whenever a favourable opportunity have offered or may offer itself.

DIVISIONS IN THE WESLEYAN BACUP CIRCUIT

A many of the old leaders in Bacup circuit have died off since 1835, and a great number have been made since who have been asked if they agree with Wesleyan Methodist's discipline; and of course, they agreed, not knowing anything about Methodist law "as it is," or was, nor do they either look after it or understand it.

I was at our quarterday at Bacup on the 3rd Oct. 1850 and mentioned the regulations passed last Conference in reference to the trial of members to several leaders that day, who knew nothing about it. I said, "Do you read nothing about these things." They said "No." I told them they were sadly neglecting their duty, but they appeared to me to be like the ostrich which runs its head into the edge, and thinks itself quite safe from all its enemies. But I thought I would do my duty at the quarterly meeting, so I moved and it was seconded by Mr. Lupton, local preacher that the regulations passed last conference in reference to the trial of members be not enforced in Bacup circuit this year." I told the meeting if this became law it would give the preachers a power which a preacher ought not to have. Leaders ought to be, and I believe are, as good men as preachers as regards honesty and piety, and one ought not to be suspected any more than the other. But suppose I was a superintendent and had a pique at some leader or member, I will tell you what I could do under that law; I could bring a charge against him, and withhold his ticket. If he demanded a trial, I could ask him to tell me whether he was guilty or not. The man might say, without giving the principle a thought, "Not guilty." Then if I had no case I could say, "Well brother, I believe you and will give you your ticket," and then look out for another opportunity. By and by I could bring another charge against him, and so on till I got him to say "No, you keep bringing charges against me and you bring no evidence forward to prove them, therefore I will not tell you whether I am guilty or not. If you have any charge bring forward your proof, and let me have a fair trial." I could then say, "The business is now settled. You are no longer a member." It was contended in the meeting that a preacher would never do a thing like that. I said "Yes, a preacher has done a worse thing than that by me in this circuit, and there are living witnesses to bear me out, and the preacher was the Rev. Thomas Davis." After this and many other things which were said Mr. Dawson, local preacher, moved an amendment to the following effect. (Though I do not remember the exact wording of the amendment). "That this meeting disapproves of the disturbance in the connection, and that it is as determined this day as ever to maintain Methodism and all its laws." I said, "Do you mean "Methodism as it is," and he said, "Yes." "Well," I said, "I am astonished." Some wanted both the motion and the amendment to be withdrawn. I said, "No, I must do my duty. I shall not withdraw my motion." And they were both put to the meeting by the Chairman. For the amendment 17 voted and for the original motion 4 voted, and as many or more were neutral. I was satisfied in what I had done, though it was painful to my mind to see so many of our leaders ignorant respecting the laws of our connection. Ignorance and unfaithfulness of the officers of the church is the reason why popery got into the Church of Rome or any other church. And nothing in my opinion can be more corrupting to the church of God than such an inquisitorial law as "questioned by penalty." A law giving the right to ask a man whether he is guilty or not of some immoral act, without bringing any witness against him or acquainting him of his accuser. If he was guilty he might as easily say "Not guilty" as commit the immoral act. But say "Not guilty", being innocent without knowing his accuser, would be to let the thief who had been robbing the accused of his character, go free without knowing him. The man asking the questions, perhaps the minister under whom the accused had sat in the house of God, might be the real thief himself. This is "Methodism as it is," which is evil speaking, to be kept secret from the object of the evil speakers malice, or from the person on whom the malice of the evil speaker has been brooding. Which lays open a door for all kinds of intrigue and clandestinely robbing a man of his character with whom the robber walks to the house of God, calling him his brother. Such an instrument as "Question by penalty" is despicable and is the offset of sin or the Devil.

If men must pledge themselves to such a law and "Methodism as it is" before they be received into office as class leader or local preacher or any other office in the connection, what kind of officers will they have in a short time when such pledges must be attended to before deep piety; and if in the least deviated from, a greater punishment awarded than for immorality. Query, can an intelligent man give the above pledge and enjoy real piety? I believe that such pledges are now common before an office is given. A very respectable gentleman in Manchester who, I believe, no man delighted more to have preachers' company than he did, told me a few months ago that he had left the Methodists and had gone over to the Church of England. I was surprised, and asked him his reason. He said, "Well, Mr. Whitehead. I have not done it without thought." They (the Methodists) wanted me to take office and give a pledge which I could not do. And near to where I live there is a very pious church minister, and I thought It would be the best for me and my family at once to go over to the church, and I have sent in my resignation to the Wesleyans and have gone.

So if "Methodism as it is" cannot be reformed, it will lose the men of great minds, fidelity and piety; if "Methodism as it is" be not reformed at this time the consequence will be awful. But if the people will not secede and pursue their present plan, they will most assuredly obtain a reform and such, in principle, laid down by the delegates. If so Methodism will go ahead of all other churches.

SIXTIETH BIRTHDAY, 11 DEC 1850

I am this day sixty years old, and my wife is in her fifty third year, by whom I have had eleven children. All of which I have suckled, nine of which are now living, the youngest near fourteen years old, and we have six grandchildren living. She is a leader of five classes of which she became the leader in the following years. viz: 1834 of her Thursday class, 1839 of her Sunday class, 1841 of her Tuesday class, 1846 of her Wednesday class, and in 1847 of her Sunday Morning class; in which classes she has to this present time meeting, 84 members and 30 on trial, in all 110. Besides which she meets a number of school children on each Sunday afternoon. Her chief delight is the salvation of immortal souls. She is a good Christian shepherd, a good mother and a good wife. It is more than 32 years since our Marriage Union; for which I thank God, and acknowledge him in his goodness and mercy which has abounded unto us. It is more than 33 years since Brothers and I commenced business as co-partners. God in his providence has made our business to prosper, and the greatest blessing of all, he has made our souls to prosper, having an interest in the blood of Christ, the forgiveness of our sins, and I trust we all do now enjoy the witness of the spirit to bear witness with our spirit, that we are his children. Glory be to God, he is the Lord of Lords, the King of Kings. The cattle upon a thousand hills are his. The silver and the Gold are his, Earth is his, and the fullness thereof; yea, the Houses and the mills we have built, and the furniture and machinery we have put into them, are all his, and we are his – for he has made us. And though we have forfeited all right to his Kingdom, he has redeemed us by his blood, and witnessed with his spirit, that we are born of God, and hath preserved us to the present time. Glory be to God for our Glorious privilege, and may we serve him in all our business, in all our factories, and with all our machinery, which are all his. All our work and all we do may be one continual service to God. Lord help me fully to avail myself of my Glorious privilege, and may I serve thee more faithful than ever I have done. I have been more than 35 years a member of thy church – 32 years a class leader. Lord pardon all my unfaithfulness; for Christ sake cleanse this heart of mine – make me just right and keep me right – work in me to will and to do of thy good pleasure. Write thy truth and thy law of love in my heart that I may love thee with all my heart and my neighbour as myself. Give me light and guide my by thy spirit that I may not side with the powerful because they are powerful, against the weak. Give me a clear understanding, and help me to be unflinchingly faithful to thy enlightening spirit, and let nothing of this world ever draw me from what is right – from "truth." Ever keep me from a desire of the honour that is of this world. May my only desire be to serve and do thy will. Many high things are to be brought low before thy Gospel can spread all over the world; if thou hast anything for me to do towards accomplishing thy will. I am thy servant, only show me how it is to be done, and help me to do my part. O God help me to answer the end for which thou made me, help me to live nearer to thee, than I ever have done, and may it be my delight to do thy will. Glory be to God. I feel a will resigned to thy will. Take me into they hands, and do with me as seemeth thee good, and save me for ever, for Christ sake.   Amen.

JUSTICE OF THE PEACE

February 25th 1851.

I have been this day officially informed that my name is inserted in the Commission of the Peace for the county Palatine of Lancaster, pursuant to a Fiat of the Right Honorable the Earl of Carlisle, Chancellor of the Duchy and County Palatine.

And on the 9th of April, 1851, I qualified for the same.

NOTES

1. Members of the Peel family were senior partners in calico printing concerns at both Bury and Church Bank, near Accrington. They employed several thousand hand loom weavers to provide their cloth.
2. The Larks of Dean (The Dean Layrocks), a famous group of amateur musicians from the hamlet of Dean in Rossendale.
3. Feizer House, a water-powered mill at Waddington, near Clitheroe, began spinning in 1793.
4. Sir John Byng (1772-1860) took part in the Peninsula campaign under Wellington. Received command of Northern Districts in 1822. Created Earl of Strafford in 1847.
5. Angelica Catalani (1780-1849), Italian bravura soprano and impresario, who commanded extravagant fees.

6. 1st edition 1841; 3rd (reprinted) edition, Cass 1968.
7. Elias Moses & Son, pioneers of the ready-made clothing industry in the East End of London. Thomas Hood's poem *The Song of the Shirt*, first published in Punch in 1844, made the sweated labour of their workers notorious.
8. James Everett, Methodist minister expelled from the Wesleyan Conference in 1849 following publication of pamphlets opposing the Conference. He was active in forming the United Methodist Free Church in 1857 and first President.
9. Samuel Dunn, Methodist minister expelled with Everett for publishing *The Wesley Banner*, later became minister of the Methodist Episcopal Church of America.
10. William Griffin JP, Methodist minister expelled with Everett and Dunn. Following these expulsions in 1849, many thousands left the Connection to join the United Methodist Free Church.
11. Pamphlets attacking the leadership of the Wesleyan Conference, thought to have been produced by Everett.

Though David Whitehead lived on until 1865, he appears not to have written about the final years of his life.

LETTERS OF DAVID WHITEHEAD AND BETTY WOOD

Longholme.
December 22nd, 1817.

Dear Betty,

I take the liberty of writing a few lines to you, and, if they meet your approbation, they will greatly accomplish my desires. I do intend to marry sooner or later, and you are at present the only one that I have in view. Your family, for anything that I have seen or heard (and inquiry I have made), does in a great degree satisfy me. So on that account I have no objections to become one of your family. I take you to be one of God's dear children which I do prefer before any other in the Kingdom. In short, I think you will suit me for a wife the best of any that I have yet noticed. I have had a great deal of meditation, thought and consideration about this matter, a matter of the greatest importance, a matter that ought to be well considered. We ought to pray to God for directions; and may you and I pray to God that if it will be for our present and eternal welfare to be married together, that it may be forwarded. And if He sees that it will not be for our good, that it may be by Him frustrated. And by so doing in sincerity God will hear us, and if it will be for our good to be married together, I have no doubt but that God, who made us, will join us together in holy matrimony.

Dear Betty, I candidly desire that you will take this into consideration; and please to have the goodness to answer this letter. When I was in your country, I had a desire to have a few hours of private conversation with you, but this apparently was impossible. So I make bold to solicit you with this letter. I sincerely love you or I would not have written unto you. So I desire you, whatever your thoughts may be upon the subjects, to write unto me. You may convey your letter by my brother. This letter leaves me anxious to have another. So I remain,

Your loving and certainly your intended husband, and if my intentions are frustrated, I shall be in Christ,

Your loving brother,

David Whitehead.

Dovesyke, December 30th, 1817.

Sir

Your addresses were very unexpected, and I, knowing but little of you, makes me very timid about writing. Had I not thought you one who loved and feared God, I should not have answered your letter.

Respecting my present state of life I feel content and satisfied, and determined not to alter till the providence of God opens the way. I often feel afraid lest I should, in a matter of such consequence, lean to my own understanding. Yet I believe if I, by prayer and watchfulness look to the Lord, in this also he will direct my path. I consider the marriage state a happy one if entered upon in the fear and with the approbation of God. Yet as I told you I think it is too soon for me to enter into this state, as I consider youth the most favourable time for the growth of religion in the soul. And to get married when so very young seems to me as if it was cropping it in the bud.

I have far from thinking, as some folks do about this, that when they get married all is over, and now they will have nothing wherewith to try them. I think the single state is the best time to get Grace, and the married one to try it. But some would object and say that untried Grace is no Grace. But I think it possible to have it though it be untried. I now conclude by saying that I will wait and see what the Lord will say concerning this matter, so I remain your friend and well-wisher in the bonds of Christian affection,

Betty Wood.

Longholme, January 20th 1818

Dear Betty,

I very gladly received your letter which affords me another opportunity of writing to you. This leaves me in good health, with love to you; and if God willing, I pray it may find you the same.

I desire that my request be granted, as follows: - Next Monday, if God willing, I shall go to Manchester, and on Tuesday take the coach from Manchester to Clithero. I think it will be ten o'clock or betwixt that and eleven before the coach reach Clithero, so that it will be eleven or twelve before I can reach brother's house. Now I desire to be in your company a little on this night, and I could not like to be disappointed, as I shall come on purpose to have some private conversation with you. Conversation on paper is suitable in its turn. But I think personal conversation is preferable in this case. Please to leave word at my brother's how I shall meet with you at your house, as I should like to see you on Tuesday night without fail; because I should return home soon in the morning. The Tuesday I mention will be the 27th of this month, then I hope I shall see you personally.

I am, your affectionate lover,
David Whitehead.

Longholme, February 4th, 1818.
Dear intended wife,

I am glad to inform you that the cough I had when I was at your house is much better, thanks be to Almighty God. I have reason to be truly thankful to God for his goodness towards me both in temporal and spiritual things. Now I pray that He Who inhabits eternity, Who is omniscient and fills immensity of space, Who is from everlasting to everlasting, His eye is over all and His knowledge as great as His fullness, His power immeasurable, – to command my heart and direct my pen that it may not be of myself but of Him that made me. I can say my desires and affections increase towards you, I feel nothing contrary to love. I love you as a partner in life; not as my Creator, God forbid that I should. We are to love one another with brotherly love but I would have you and I to surpass this, so that we should be two happy companions through all our journey to another and better world, to be sincere friends, pleasant companions, faithful partners, and useful assistants to each other.

"So that if we met with difficulties by the way, to take each other by the hand for support.

In dangers, to counsel and stand by each other.

In sorrow to sympathise and comfort one another.

If beset with enemies, one to watch while the other slept.

If one were sick, the other to comfort with cordials.

If one was indisposed in mind, the other to divert with some sweet song or discourse concerning another world.

If one were at a loss concerning any part of the way, the other to assist in searching and explaining the directions.

If one were ready to turn aside, the other to caution and admonish of the danger.

If one were employed in any service, the other to be ready to assist therein.

If one found a refreshing spring by the way, the other to come and drink.

If one found any refreshing fruit, sweet spices or delightful flowers, to pluck and bring to the other.

If one heard any joyful tidings, to come rejoicing and tell the other.

And if one was blessed with any special favours, the other may congratulate and rejoice. &c."

When we should prove that two are better than one. I feel quite satisfied in my mind for you to be thus my partner in life, and that we may be thus united together, so that it may be that two are become one. Now as I tell you my mind so freely, I should like an answer equally so. For I think it is not good to carry on things of this kind far, except they be both be of one mind, nor to enter upon them too rashly. But, may the Lord direct you and I that our steps may be sure.

From Your affectionate and intended husband
David Whitehead

P.S. I got very well home but not till Thursday morning. On Wednesday I stopped all night at Burnley. When I shall come again I cannot tell in this letter, perhaps I shall tell you in the next. Please to tell me in your next letter whether anybody had any knowledge of my last visit, except you and my brother.

Dovesyke, February 16th 1818.

Dear Sir,

I received your letter on Tuesday morning last, and am glad to know that you got well home, and that the Lord blesses you with health of body, and I trust health of soul too. O, how thankful we ought to be for all his mercies conferred upon us! I at present have a very severe cold which makes me rather unwell, but this I can say, I feel my soul alive to God, and I feel I love Him above every other object.

Since I saw you last I have considered much about the solemn engagement of marriage, and I have also made it a matter of much prayer to God. And with thankfulness, I can say with respect thereto, that I feel resigned to the will of God, and a determination by His help to follow the guidance of His spirit as I trust I have hitherto done.

I have lately been reading the several duties of husbands and wives by Mr. Wesley, duties which I think ought to be known and performed by all married people. And if ever I marry I should like to have, and answer, the character described in your letter. But of myself I feel very inadequate to the task. Yet through Christ strengthening me I can do all things. And should the Lord see it meet, of twain to make us one, I have no doubt but if our works in him be wrought, they shall be blessed indeed. But in my opinion a work of so difficult a nature should not be hastily undertaken. I think we ought duly to consider and carefully to watch the movings of the spirit of God herein, for hasty marriages often prove unhappy ones. Such, I hope, neither you nor I will ever have to experience. I ever now recommend myself to the blessing of God and to your prayers. Assuring you of an interest in mine.

> From, yours in affection,
> Betty Wood.

P.S. I believe nobody knew anything about your visit the last time, except myself and your brother.

> Longholme, February 28th 1818.

Dear intended wife,

I have just received your letter which I can truly say has done my soul good, and increased my affection towards you. I can assure you that I often pray for you; and feel my soul blessed when engaged in this delightful duty. Prayer is food for my soul.

May God grant that I may ever pray, without fainting. I desire to be such an one as God is willing; and that, I may not be of myself, but that His will should be done in me. I am inclined to think that it is God's will for you to become my partner in life; and if it should be so, I hope we shall be shortly happily joined together.

Last Tuesday night I was in company with a good old friend of mine, a Quaker, who after a little conversation, said to me, "Thou must get married. By all means get thee married," says he. "Hast thou no one in thy mind?"

I could not easily give the good old man an indirect answer, so I told him that I had. He asked if she was of the same religion as me. I said she was. He said, "Be sure thou get married to her," and when I was going to leave him, he said, "Well, are thou going to see this woman this week?" I said, "I think not this week." "When did thou see her?" said he.

I told him, about a month ago. He said, "She will wonder what thou art doing. When does thou intend to go?" I said, "I cannot tell." "Well, but I would go and make it up," said he.

I have been thinking myself that it would be as well for me to be married, but I intend to come over sometime in the course of a fortnight or thereabouts. Then you and I can have some talk about these things. I am very glad to hear from you, but feel sorry that you have such a bad cold. At the same time hoping this will find you well as it leaves me at present. So I pray God may keep you and I while on earth, and that we may reign with him as long as eternal ages roll.

    I remain, your loving and intended husband,
      David Whitehead.

  The Love of God
  Could we with ink the ocean fill,
  Were the whole earth of parchment made,
  Were every single stick a quill,
  And every man a scribe by trade
  To write the love of God above
  Would drain the ocean dry,
  Nor could the scrawl contain the whole.
  Though stretched from sky to sky.

        Dovesyke, March 17th 1818.
Dear David,
  Agreeable to your request, I sit down with pleasure to inform you that on Monday next, God willing, I intend coming to Bury. The young woman I mentioned to you is coming with me. My father will bring us in the cart to near Accrington, and then we shall walk forward to Bury. We intend taking Silverwood Coach to Manchester the following morning. Now I should like to see you on one of these days, for I think it will be the only opportunity I shall have of being in your company. I think it will be better for you not to come to the house where I shall be at, in Manchester. I have not time at present to tell you my reasons why I think so. My father and mother takes it better over you than I expected they would have done, but before you write to my father, I want to have a deal of talk with you.
  I have not yet received your letter but I hope I shall in a day or two. This letter leaves me in good health, and my soul in a good measure alive to God, and hope it will find you, my dear David, the same.
    I remain, my dearly beloved,
      Your true lover,
        Betty Wood.

Longholme, 19th March, 1818.

My dear intended wife,

This morning I very gladly received your letter. I feel thankful to God that you are in good health of body and your soul alive to God. I shall be glad if I can meet with you on the road next Monday. I intend to be on the road betwixt Haslingden and Accrington about ten o'clock next Monday morning; and if not meeting you, shall be at Accrington about eleven o'clock, and will stop if not seeing you, till about twelve. So I hope I shall see you on Monday, which will give me great pleasure. If not I shall see you at Bury on Tuesday morning.

I thankfully inform you that I am in good health at present, and can truly say that God doth greatly bless my soul. Last Thursday night I went to my class meeting. While singing, the Class Leader stepped back and asked me to go to his son's Class, his son not being well. I felt inadequate to the task, and my mind much indisposed. Yet I went, and found God to be strength in weakness, and wonderfully to bless my soul. While talking to the members, I felt great liberty. I felt as if I would be such an one as God would have me to be; and that if I could be instrumental to the good of any soul, that he might bless my labours. That it might be not of myself but of him, who is the giver of all good gifts. In short, God is goodness and mercy to me, and I pray that you and I may enjoy the presence of God at all times.

    I remain, yours in affection and am, my dear,
        Your real lover and intended husband,
            David Whitehead.

Longholme, 16th April, 1818

My dear intended wife,

Please to deliver this letter to your father. I shall be glad to hear from you soon, and what your father says concerning us.

I got well home on Wednesday night, and am in pretty good health at present, thank God for it. If your father ask you when we intend to be married, tell him in about a month. You know it is a long way for me to come. I think we had better be married soon. I have told my mother, as I thought it was my duty. She says she is very glad and advises me to be married soon. I am not writing much, you know my mind.

    From your intended husband,
        Whose love and affections are the same,
            David Whitehead.

[To Mr. Wood]
Longholme, 16th April, 1818.

Dear Sir,

I take liberty to solicit you as an intended father, and if my solicitations meet your approbation, they will greatly accomplish my desires. Perhaps you may be much surprised, having little knowledge of the correspondence betwixt your daughter and me. I think it my duty to inform you the first time I saw your daughter to my knowledge was on Sunday, the 14th of December last. I noticed her more than others. On Monday night I told her my intentions, and desired her to consider them. Shortly after I sent her a letter, and received an answer. Since then we have been corresponding with each other several times, so that we are, I believe, one in heart and affections. You may think that our intimacy is very short. Short it is, but sincere. Our hearts are so united to each other that it is impossible for man to separate them, so I humbly beg that you will give her me to wife. In a short time I should like to be married, but not without your consent. I don't think it wisdom to marry rashly, without consideration, nor yet to drive it too long when affections are great and sincere lest mortal affections corrupt the immortal soul, and weaken the love of God in the heart. God forbid it should. I am truly thankful that can say since I began to keep company with your daughter, that it has not been destructive to the grace of God in me, but, I think, an increase. When I see the various and dangerous temptations to which I have been exposed, it leads me to praise God that he has found me one that has an interest in Christ; for I feel of myself weak, and have no need of one to weaken but to strengthen me in the grace of God till glory shall end what grace has begun. We think it is the will of God for us to be partners in life. Prayers have been offered unto God on that account, and we think nothing has been done without His approbation.

I shall be glad to receive an answer from you, that you are willing likewise yet I must own you a father to me in matters of this kind. Therefore give me instructions as a child.

    My love to you and your wife.
        Desiring to become your dutiful and happy son.
        David Whitehead.

P.S. shall be glad to have an answer as soon as you can make it convenient.

Longholme, 30th April, 1818.

Very dear intended wife,

I received a letter from Brother this morning, and fully expected one from you, but my brother informed me in his letter that you had not had time to write. I am glad to hear from you in any way, but through the love which I have towards you it feels more pleasing to hear from your own hand than by another. Perhaps it may be the same with you, so I enclose a few lines.

My dear, I am very well at present, hoping that you are the same, for which we ought to give God the praise. If you can make it convenient to write to me next week, I shall gladly accept the letter; and tell me what your father says, and what you think about us being married. If I get a letter next week, I shall send another to you by return of coach on Thursday, and can perhaps tell you when I shall come over. Then I should like you to make up your mind when to be married, if in case your father is willing. My dear, I cannot say much to you at present, having so little time to write.

From yours in affection, and am, my dear,
Your loving intended husband,
David Whitehead.

Dovesyke, 6th May, 1818

Dear David

I very gladly received your last on Friday night, and the other letters on the Friday before, and your brother gave the letter to my father on Saturday morning. When he read it he was very much affected as was also my mother, and I leave you to judge what my feelings were for they are better felt than described. But I laid my case before the Lord, and I found him to strengthen and help me, and cause me to stand upheld, by his omnipotent hand.

I expected my father would have had a deal to say to me about being married, but to my great surprise he has never said a word, one way nor another. My mother says she has nothing against me being married if it was to one I knew something more about, but she thinks I know but little either of your character or your circumstance; and I leaving home so far, she knows not how to bear it. So you may think I have had many crosses and trials to encounter, but I have found God to be my present help in every time of need. This promise has been a wonderful support to my soul, ("Fear not, I am with thee be not dismayed for I am thy God"). I feel I can say in all things, "The will of the Lord be done." I believe it is the providence of God that has thus far brought us together, and his will that we should be more closely joined. If so, I have no doubt but we shall be blessed together; while in time, and at the last reign with him in glory.

It gives me great pleasure to hear that you are well as this leaves me at present, and I shall expect one from you by return of coach.

From yours with sincere and increasing affections.
Betty Wood.

P.S. Your brother would have you to send when the house will be ready, and he says he believes the letter had not been opened.

Longholme, 7th May, 1818.
Very dear intended wife,

I very gladly received your letter this morning, and am thankful to hear that you are well as this leaves me at present; and may He who gives the health have the praise. My dear, I feel for you on account of the exercise of your mind, through what your mother has said to you concerning your having so little knowledge about me. It is every parent's duty to see after the welfare of their children, so we should not think they are hard with us on that account. For all they say to us is most likely intended for our present and eternal welfare. I can truly say, my dear, that I should be very glad indeed if we were married. But I should like to be reconciled to your father and mother. It is right that they should know my character, and, if it was not agreeable, not to accept me.

But you know I cannot recommend myself. If I should paint myself in its own colour, it perhaps might not please; for I know more vileness of myself than those who are the most acquainted with me.

I should have been glad to have written more to you, but I have not time today. I shall come over the first opportunity. Perhaps it way not be before next Tuesday but one, then I shall be at Manchester; and if I come not before, I intend to come to your house that night. If I come before, I intend to be at your house by ten o'clock. If I could have come tonight instead of writing, I would, for I am not content from you. I am in haste. So may you and I trust in God and we shall not be confounded.

I am, your loving and intended husband,
David Whitehead.

P.S. If your father says anything to you, please to drop a line next Thursday, if I come not before. I will come if convenient.

Dovesyke, 27th May, 1818.

My dear David,

With pleasure I sit down to write to you, and am happy to say I feel the presence of the Lord to overshadow me while I write. But, respecting us being married at the time you mentioned, I scarce know what to say. Since you left me, I have often laid the matter before God in prayer and trust you have done the same. I have had a deal of talk with my mother, and she is more reconciled about it than before. But my father said nothing, and I have not courage to begin first. My mother says she thinks he is not willing to go with you for a license, and next Wednesday he has to go to Blackburn. So I think if you come as proposed you will not have an opportunity of seeing him, except it be soon in the morning.

I have thought we had better not be married till after I am at age which will be about eight weeks. But in this I would do the will of God. May He direct and guide us that we may do all in His appointed time, and then we are sure of his blessing. But if you think it better to be married at the time mentioned, you had better write to my father and state some of your reasons for it being so soon and when you intend seeing him. And may He who has the hearts of all men in His hand direct you: and then you will not err.

My dear love, I now leave these things to your better consideration, and the blessing of God. Hoping this letter will find you in good health as it leaves me at present. I shall most gladly expect to hear from you by return of coach.

   From yours in true and sincere affections,
   Betty Wood.

P.S. If you write to my father, I should like you to send the letter as before.

Longholme, 28th May, 1818.

Dear intended wife

I this morning received your letter and I take a delight in writing to you, but with regard to answering it, I scarcely know how, having so little time to consider about it, and being so busily engaged in other things. When I got home from my last visit to you, it was told me that two or three persons had been trying to take the mill which we have, but have not yet obtained their end. I am trying to stop them, which I hope by the help of God I shall, if it be for my good. I desire in all things to be directed by the Almighty.

I have been also offering to take three cottage houses today. I have not yet taken them but have them in my choice, whether to take them or not. I mention these things in order to inform you how my mind is exercised, and I desire an interest in your prayers. I am venturing hard, and if I must do business, I must venture.

I am not writing to your father today, because I have nothing particular to state to him, only, you know, that I should like to be married soon, on one account. We are so far distant from each other, and I think, the sooner and the better, as I trust our affections to each other are sincere. But sooner than it should be so very inconvenient, I would rather put it off a little, but you know you can talk with your mother about it. You can consider about it till next Tuesday night. I think it is good to adhere to more experienced people than ourselves. So you can see what your mother or father say about it. I should wish to do all things in peace and in such order as will give satisfaction to all if possible.

From your loving and affectionate
intended husband,
David Whitehead.

P.S. If in case I do not come on Tuesday night next, you may think something has turned out unexpected. If I come I shall be at your house soon after twelve if not before. I am very well. In haste.

Dovesyke, 29th May, 1818.

Dear expected husband,

I this morning received your letter, and I believe I more fully understand the meaning of our Lord where he says "And they twain shall be made one" than I ever did before for truly I can say I bear a share with you. The first opportunity I laid your case before God in prayer, and have not a doubt but the Lord will make your way plain before you. For while engaged on your account I found my soul blessed and encouraged. With respect to us being married, I have no doubt if we look to Him we shall be directed to the best time.

From yours in true and sincere affections,
Betty Wood.

Dovesyke, 10th June, 1818.

Dear expected husband,

I feel thankful to God that I have the pleasure of writing to you, not doubting but you will feel equal pleasure in receiving. For no other motive than pure love hath induced me to act as I have done, and I believe it is the same with you.

The day after you went home I told my mother that you had been, and when we intended being married. She talked with me very quietly about it. On Monday your brother asked my father leave, I expect he will tell you the answer he got the same day. My mother told my father when we were for being married, and asked him about us having the dinner at home; and I believe he has nothing against it. They both seem better reconciled than I expected they would have been. But this I believe is the Lord's doing, and it is marvellous in our eyes.

My dear, we are about to enter into a most important state in life; we shall stand in need of much of the grace of God. I have often felt while engaged in prayer on this account the Lord to bless me, and I have no doubt but we shall be helpmeets one to another. I hope we shall not cease to pray to God for his blessing upon what we are about to do, and then our prayers will ascend and meet at the throne of grace and find acceptance there.

This letter leaves me in good health as I trust it will find you, for I feel as much interest in your health and welfare as that of my own, for I believe the happiness of one consists in the happiness of the other. I shall expect seeing you in a week or a fortnight from this time, and I think it better not to write before, except you have something particular to say. I now solicit an interest in your prayers. and remain,

    Your loving and intended wife,
    Betty Wood.

          Dovesyke, 13th June, 1818.
Dear David,

I expect you will be a little surprised on the reception of this letter, but not more than it leaves me. On Friday night my father met with my uncle Joseph, as he was coming back, and he told him that you said that you were giving up the shop to your brother, you were so far off. But you thought if you continued partners, you and your sister would remove to the place sometime. When he (my father) came home, he began to tell my mother about it, and he expected you intended me living with you, and weaving; or else you were making a fool of me altogether. I told them you had taken a house, I believed, and were not thinking of any such things. But with this I was no better, for they said if you had, you either thought of me living in a cottage house to weave, or work in the mill, and you were marrying me from some motive that was not good. Such a night and day have I passed as I never did before; for if things be as they say they are, you have been deceiving me.

Soon after our acquaintance you told me that you had a shop and had not time to attend to it yourself, and wanted me to help you in it. Now you have never told me anything to the contrary. Of course I have expected nothing to the contrary. You know very well you have gained my affections, and I have loved you most sincerely. But if things be as I am told they are, I will give all up though it cost me my life. But Oh! what are my feelings in respect to this? Them, I can never describe. We have been making every preparation for us to be married, our folks say they were reconciled to it; but if what my uncle say be true, they are as far to the contrary, and say they never can think well of you again. So you must not get the licence nor think of me being married till I hear more about it.

I think it my duty thus to write to you whether what I hear be true or not. I now conclude with saying, "The will of the Lord be done."; for I feel a will resigned to His will. May He ever keep it so, prays

     Yours distressed lover
     Betty Wood.

P.S. I shall expect to see you or hear from you on Monday night.

         Longholme, 20th June, 1818.
Dear Betty,

I received your letter on Friday last, at which I am wonderfully surprised. I feel at present as if I could not tell how to write to you, but I beg leave to write to you as plain as possible. I don't think that I ever mentioned my sister living at Balladen at all. Perhaps I might mention that I intended to live there myself, if in case that we could agree with Mr. Hargreaves over the mill. For Mr. Hargreaves wants more rent than we shall give; so we have not taken the mill yet, nor are we certain that we shall take it. And as to turning the shop over to my brother, that is impossible, for it is belonging to one as much as another. Only them that wait upon the shop will receive something for their trouble. As for brothers dissolving partnership, we never intend so long as we do business. I do not know how your uncle might understand us, I am not aware we gave him a hint, in the least, that you and I were going to be married. So he might take things different to what we might think. I cannot tell how it is that your parents think that I want you, as they intimate, to be my slave. You know if I want people to work in the mill, I can get them for paying them a wage. So I need not get a wife for such uses as those.

I do intend to keep my wife, not as a servant but as a wife. They likewise suppose that my motive is not good; in what way they think it is not good I cannot tell. You said in your last letter it was nothing but pure love that caused you to act as you were doing. It certainly is real love that has or does induce me to pay any regards towards you. For if it were for any other motive than love, I could marry in my own country. But when I marry, I intend to marry for love in reality.

Now I don't wish to deceive you, you ought to consider we may have a fair start at the first, and may be rough all the way afterwards. You know it is all in the hands of Providence. For my part, I can say, "His will and not mine." I am at present, and have been for several years back, able to maintain more than you and myself; and I hope, by God's assistance I still shall be. You know, it may be that I may be rich of worldly goods, or that I may be extremely poor. We ought to consider whether our love will stand in adversity or not; if so, we may marry, if not, we had better decline.

This feels very arch for me to write, but though it be, you have compelled me so to write. I feel my mind so agitated at present that I cannot express myself as I would do. But after all, I must own that my love towards you is more than I thought it had been, for had it not been great I should not have felt so much anxiety of mind as I do at present. Had it not been for love, your letter would not have caused me one moment of trouble, for you cannot comfort me with anything but yourself; because I have good clothing, provisions, a house as good as I could wish for, and attended on as well as perhaps I ever must be; money in business certainly is good, and if in case we want more, I have no doubt but we have friends that will help us. So it is real love that now induces me to write to you. Had it not been for love, I would not have taken my pen to write at all. If I want to marry for money I can have it in the neighbourhood. But before I marry for money I will remain as I am, for I am well off. But if I get someone that I do not like, and cannot get rid of her, I shall be badly off. And as I am well off, I desire to be truly thankful to God for all

His mercies, for His mercy and goodness have followed me all the days of my life.

I cannot say, Betty, that I should like to give it up except it be the Lord's will. And if it be, the marriage will stop without doubt; and if not, I think it will go forward. But I intend to be at your house on Monday night next, if all be well. Then I shall be glad to see you, and if you have not as much love for me as you had, I cannot help it.

I could as soon have thought of anything as the letter I have received from you, so I cannot tell how you may be changed. The last that received from you was written on the 10th inst., and this that I have received now, on the 13th inst – which appears to be so much different to the former.

I have told some of my dear friends that I intended to be married very soon. I love to be a man in all I say, that is: that what I say, to be so in reality. You may certainly think that if I am a man of sense, I am grieved, and when I come I should like you to be able to give me an answer, in reality what you intend to do. Now I would have you to rue in time, not after we are married; and if you feel the least of rue in your mind, I would have us to decline at once. Because my mind was fully settled concerning us being married, leaving all other things to the Almighty. But, however, it is your option at present.

I still remain,
Your real lover,
David Whitehead.

P.S. I fix on 9 o'clock to be at your house. It may be an hour or sooner or an hour or two later.

Dovesyke 1st July, 1818.

My dear expected husband,

It is with unspeakable pleasure I take my pen to write to you, but having been unexpectedly called from home this morning I shall be under the painful necessity of writing very short, which I hope you will excuse. Yesterday my father was at Mitton and saw the Minister, and he says you may depend upon him being at home on Tuesday morning. I have also talked with Joseph Barnes, and he will be at Mitton by eight o'clock as before; and if he is there before you, he will come on the road till he meet you. But if you are there first, I think you had better stop at the inn on your right hand as you come before you reach the bridge, and then you may wait for him.

I mentioned to my cousin about your brother Peter coming, but she says she does not know how his coming to their house will please, so I think he had better stop at Waddington. My father says he would rather we went to John Pillings, at the Sign of the Buck, Waddington.

My dear, I still feel God is with me and blesses me with health of body and mind; and I trust you enjoy the same blessings. But I must conclude, and

I remain yours in sincere affection, and believe me, yours with all the endearments of a wife,

Betty Wood.

FUNERAL OF D. WHITEHEAD, ESQ.

Yesterday, the mortal remains of this much lamented gentleman were conveyed to their last resting place in the family vault, in the Longholme chapel burial ground. About eleven o'clock in the forenoon the various tradesmen in the town closed their shops in token of their respect for the deceased, and large numbers assembled to witness the funeral *cortege* as it passed from Holly Mount to the chapel, order being kept among the crowd by Mr. Superintendent Jervis. The procession, which started about twelve, was headed by two mutes, then followed several magistrates and ministers, next the hearse, and then the mourners. At the entrance to the chapel-yard the Rev. J. S. Withington took the lead, reading the burial service, and upon entering the chapel the Dead March in Saul was performed on the organ by P. H. Whitehead, Esq. in a very effective manner. The corpse was placed in front of the pulpit, and the attendants at the funeral sat immediately before it; the rest of the body of the chapel being occupied by the operatives late in the employ of the deceased. The Rev. J. S. Withington then stood up in the pulpit, and read the second portion of the burial service in a deeply impressive manner. While this was being done the utmost stillness prevailed, and from all parts of the chapel sobbing was audibly heard. At the close, the procession was re-formed, and the body deposited in the vault. The third part of the burial service was then read, and several of the relatives and friends of the deceased descended the vault in order to take a last look at the coffin. The plate bore the inscription:—"David Whitehead, died 26th Jan., 1865, aged 74." A numerous body of friends, in addition to the immediate relatives of the deceased were present. Thus has ended the career of D. Whitehead, Esq., the architect of his own fortune, and the friend of the people.

Haslingden and Rawtenstall Express, February, 1865

INDEX

A
Accrington, 80, 118, 191, 192
Anti-Corn Law League, 133, 134, 137, 148, 149
apprentice, 15, 17
Ashworth James, 18, 26, 27, 144
Auxbridge, Lord, 29
Auxiliary Bible Society, 100

B
Bacup, 33, 57, 61, 68, 69, 82, 87, 88, 90, 92, 98, 99, 100, 108, 109, 122, 131, 165, 175, 176, 179
Bacup Circuit, 61, 87, 98, 99, 100, 108
Balladen, 53, 62, 199
Balladen Class, 62
Balladenbrook, 40, 41, 42, 43, 45, 53, 54, 55, 57, 58, 59, 78, 133
Barnes, Joseph, 201
Bellthorne, 25
Beverley, 91
Blackburn, 14, 16, 18, 20, 21, 80, 196
Blackpool, 28
Blackwall, 171
Blakey, Lionel, 45
Bolton, 84, 85, 88
Boothfold, 14, 15, 18
Bradford, 49, 53
Bradford Chapel, 51
Brailsford, W, 100, 104
Bramley, 90

Bramwell, William, 52
Bridgend, 58, 78
Brock Clough, 5
Brussels, 171, 172
Bunting, Jabez, 154
Burnley, 3, 14, 31, 41, 57, 81, 82, 144, 189
Bury, 23, 75, 82, 191, 192
Byng, Sir John, 83, 84

C
Canada, 98, 105, 122, 124, 129, 131, 133, 138, 139, 140
Capel Curig, 24
Catalani, Madame, 91
Ceiriog Moor Inn, 28
Chatterton, 81
Chester, 22, 28
Chirk, 28
cholera, 151, 152
Clegg, John, 35, 39
Clegg, William, 40
Clitheroe, 16, 32, 39, 49, 187
coal pits, 4, 82
Cobden, Richard, 152
Cooke Taylor, William, 134
Corn Law, 124, 130, 133, 134, 137, 148, 149, 162, 165
Crawshawbooth, 116, 167

D
Dawson, Edmund, 99
Dawson, William, 62, 68, 71, 73, 88, 90

INDEX

Dean Clough, 107
Dean singers, 27
Denbighshire, 28
Dovesyke, 52, 187, 189, 191, 194, 196, 197, 198, 201
Dublin, 28, 134

E
Economist, The, 159, 160, 161, 162

F
Factory Bill, 155, 156
Fallbarn, 47
Feaserhouse, 32, 35, 39, 41, 42, 50, 53
Fielden Brothers, 82
Fire, 127
Flannels, weaving, 7, 11
Flaxmoss, 92
Free Trade, 124, 134, 148, 152
Frodsham, 92

G
Gambleside, 3
gas works, 110
Goodshaw Chapel, 27, 117, 118
Goodshawfold, 99
Greenlaw, 13
Griffith, 172

H
Halifax, 76
Hall Hill, 55, 57, 65, 67, 68, 69, 84, 99, 100, 102, 103, 110
Hall, John, 15
Hand loom weavers, 25, 31, 34, 86
Harrison, William, 87
Harrogate, 91
Hartley, John, 55, 59

Haslingden, 14, 25, 57, 60, 61, 81, 83, 84, 92, 117, 192
Haslingden circuit, 92
Heap, William, 76
Heaton, Thomas, 133
Helmshore, 81, 119
Higher Mill, 61, 78, 110, 126
Holly Mount, 106, 107, 110, 111, 116, 126, 128, 129, 131, 134, 139, 154, 159, 160, 170, 171, 172
Holly Mount School, 116
Holt, Miser, 117, 118, 119
House of Lords, 149, 150, 152, 154
Howorth, Thomas, 34, 110
Hoyle, Thomas, 21, 45, 47, 48, 54, 60
Hull, 90, 91
Hurst Green, 52

I
Ingham, George, 18

J
Jersey, 47

K
Kay, John, 99
Kay, Thomas, 31, 57, 61
Kay, Whitehead and Co., 98, 139
Kernioge Moor, *see* Ceirog Moor

L
Lancaster, 3, 82, 86
Leeds, 90, 153, 177
Leicester, 100, 102
Liverpool, 4, 105, 119, 141, 163
London, 24, 28, 55, 60, 61, 65, 116, 129, 149, 153, 154, 156, 160, 161, 171, 172, 178

INDEX

Longholme, 31, 32, 33, 34, 35, 39, 43, 57, 61, 63, 76, 81, 82, 87, 90, 98, 99, 100, 108, 131, 136, 144, 186, 187, 188, 190, 192, 193, 194, 195, 196, 199
Lord, Samuel, 48
Loveclough, 117
Lower Mill, 110, 122, 127
Lower Rawtenstall Mill, 166

M
Manchester, 20, 21, 28, 36, 45, 47, 48, 54, 57, 65, 66, 67, 68, 69, 75, 77, 81, 84, 85, 91, 148, 151, 153, 154, 167, 182, 187, 191, 195
Meadowhead, 3
Methodism, 52, 108, 109, 144, 154, 173, 174, 176, 178, 181, 182
Metternich, 171, 174, 175
militia, 19
Mitton, 201
Montreal, 98, 105, 129, 131, 133, 140
Moorehouse, James, 37, 55
Morpeth, Lord, 154
Moses, Elias, 157
Munn, John, 21, 67, 69, 71, 75, 76, 77
Munn, Robert and Co., 82
Musbury, 5, 27

N
Nelson, Lord, 4
New Inn (Blackburn), 15
New Inn (Haslingden), 81
Newchurch, 15, 32, 34, 35, 40, 43, 48, 57, 61, 68, 69, 99, 100, 103, 131
Newhallhey Bridge, 21, 64
Northwich, 25

O
Old Clough, 82
Ormerod, Miss, 11, 12, 13, 134, 136

P
Padiham, 107
Paris Peace Congress, 171
Parliament, 28, 102, 137, 149
Peace Society, 171
Peel, Sir Robert, 160
Peel, Yates & Co., 26
Pendle Forest, 25
Pendle Hill, 49
Pickup, John, 5
Pickup Bank, 25
Pilling, John, 202
Plug Drawing Riots, 136
power looms, 78, 80, 81, 82, 83, 86, 110, 165, 170
Preston, 17

Q
Quaker, 45 190

R
racing, 120
Radicalism, 132
railway, 119, 121, 124, 126, 149, 156, 158, 159, 161, 162, 165, 171
Rakefoot Chapel, 99
Ramsbottom, 82
Rawtenstall, 14, 18, 21, 28, 47, 58, 61, 64, 66, 69, 73, 76, 78, 81, 85, 87, 94, 98, 99, 100, 102, 104, 105, 106, 110, 113, 122, 128, 131, 134, 136, 144, 154, 159, 160, 171, 177
Ribchester, 49, 52
Richard Cobden, 171
riots, 80, 81, 82, 83

INDEX

roads, 21, 156
Rochdale, 5
Rochdale Circuit, 69
Rossendale, 3, 23, 24, 117
Russell, Lord John, 153
Ruthin, 23, 24

S
Savings, 113, 114, 116
Shawforth, 69
Shrewsbury, Mr., 128, 134
spinning jenny, 40
Stacksteads, 116
Star Inn, 21
Stockport, 40, 154
Stott and Smith, 138
Sunnyside, 64

T
Tadcaster, 90
Tattersall, John, 13
Temperance Society, 114, 124, 148, 157
Todmorden, 57, 82, 105
toll bars, 73, 125
Tranter, W, 108
Turner, William, 81, 119
Twiston, 49

W
Waddington, 202
Wales, 21, 22, 23, 28
warping, 32, 34, 35, 42, 43, 57
water engine, 126
water wheel, 40, 110
Waterbarn, 82
Watkins, Major, 84
weft engine, 55, 57, 58
Wellington, Duke of, 149
Wesley, John, 3, 109, 176
Wesleyan Methodist, 39, 109
Wesleyan Times, 171, 174
West Bradford, 52
Whitehead, James, 3
Whitehead, Peter, 3, 36, 41
Whitehead, Thomas, 4, 5, 31, 32, 35, 39, 41, 42, 50, 51, 53, 55, 57, 60, 70, 73, 98, 104
Whitewell Bottom, 5, 18, 25, 31
Wood, Betty, 54
Wrexham, 28

Y
York Minster, 91